Swallowing the Sea

Also by Lee Upton

FICTION
The Guide to the Flying Island

POETRY
The Invention of Kindness
No Mercy
Approximate Darling
Civilian Histories
Undid in the Land of Undone

CRITICAL PROSE
Jean Garrigue: A Poetics of Plenitude
Obsession and Release: Rereading the Poetry of Louise Bogan
The Muse of Abandonment: Origin, Identity, Mastery in Five American Poets
Defensive Measures: The Poetry of Niedecker, Bishop, Glück, and Carson

Swallowing the Sea

On Writing & Ambition Boredom Purity & Secrecy

Lee Upton

TP

TUPELO PRESS
NORTH ADAMS, MASSACHUSETTS

Swallowing the Sea.
Copyright 2012 Lee Upton. All rights reserved.

Library of Congress Cataloging-in-Publication Data
Upton, Lee, 1953–
Swallowing the sea : on writing & ambition, boredom, purity & secrecy/Lee Upton.—1st ed.
    p. cm.
Includes bibliographical references.
ISBN 978-1-936797-13-4 (pbk. : alk. paper) –
ISBN 978-1-936797-14-1 (hardcover : alk. paper)
1. Authorship. 2. Creation (Literary, artistic, etc.)–Psychological aspects. I. Title.
PN149.U68 2012
808.02--dc23

2012020328

Cover and text designed by Howard Klein
Cover photograph: "Hawaii Wave" by John Lehet (www.lehet.com).
Used with permission of the artist.

First edition: July 2012.

Tupelo Press
P.O. Box 1767
243 Union Street, Eclipse Mill, Loft 305
North Adams, Massachusetts 01247
Telephone: (413) 664–9611 / Fax: (413) 664–9711
editor@tupelopress.org/www.tupelopress.org

Tupelo Press is an award-winning independent literary press that publishes fine fiction, nonfiction, and poetry in books that are a joy to hold as well as read. Tupelo Press is a registered 501(c)3 non-profit organization, and we rely on public support to carry out our mission of publishing extraordinary work that may be outside the realm of large commercial publishers. Financial donations are welcome and are tax deductible.

ART WORKS.
arts.gov
Supported in part by an award from the National Endowment for the Arts

—in memory of Lana Upton Kaltz

Contents

Purity

Bigamy for Beginners

Secrecy

AMBITION

Let's Start With Panic

The first story of panic: In Tomas Tranströmer's prose poem "The Name," a man pulls his car off the road, crawls into the backseat, and falls asleep. After he wakes he can't remember who he is: "I am something that wakens in a backseat, twists about in panic like a cat in a sack." Finally, the man remembers his name. This is how the poem ends:

> But impossible to forget the fifteen-second struggle in the hell of oblivion, a few meters from the main road, where the traffic glides past with its lights on.

A second story of panic, and one of the most haunting depictions of what it means to lack an inner life: Anton Chekhov's "The Darling." At first the story seems to be about a harmless woman. Young, beautiful, and willing to parrot others' opinions, initially she attracts friends and admirers. In the course of the story she takes on the views of each of her successive husbands, repeating his convictions until, widowed and alone, she fastens upon a ten-year-old boy. The story reveals the burden the child carries as the woman assumes his internal reality as her own. At the story's conclusion, the boy cries out in his sleep: "I'll give it to you! Get away! Shut up!"

Tranströmer's figure who wakes in his car is only momentarily at a loss, but his lapse points to the precariousness of identity. Chekhov's short story is about a woman's life-long failure to develop any self-reflection, or any residue of self-knowledge. It's not so much the story of an idiot as of a vampire, albeit a hapless one.

The amnesia in the first narrative is unwilled. In the second story the woman suffers a worse predicament. She doesn't comprehend her hollowness, her inability to create an identity of her own. Reflexively she preys on others to give herself a sensation of reality. Only the child victim can begin, at least in his dreams, to recognize that he is being feasted on by a succuba.

ξ

This is a book about ambition. The ambition that I know best is writerly ambition, and its peculiarities. The writer knows that he or she writes for the man waking up in the car who can't remember who he is, as well as for the child whose inner life is being invaded. The writer writes, too, for "the darling" who needs to discover her own inner resources. The writer writes against panic. And this is a book about reclaiming the writer's ambition, that idiosyncratic drive.

Certainly there are writers who are ambitious for conventional rewards, such as fame, love, money, power … although of all ways to win any of those rewards, writing would seem to be one of the most labor intensive and uncertain. Yet there's another form of ambition that writers may focus on: the ambition to make a lifetime's work that adds to the sum of what Wallace Stevens, referring to poetry, called one of the "enlargements of life." To make the written work itself more powerful—to renew ambition within the process of creating the work—is one of the most daunting of ambitions. When T. S. Eliot referred to "a raid on the inarticulate," he chose a word less likely to refer to his character Prufrock than to a Viking. Imaginative writing is a raid, and a raid on, among other riches, the writer's own resources.

Percy Bysshe Shelley was ambitious for poets as "unacknowledged legislators of the world." Generally people who read that phrase can't resist playing with the wording: acknowledge your legislators as they level the world; legislate knowledge in the underworld; ours is a world legislated by underknowledge. In his poem "Disasters," George Oppen reworked the phrase memorably into "legislators // of the unacknowledged // world."

In *The Case for Greatness: Honorable Ambition and Its Critics*, Robert Faulkner argues that "if the aims are honorable and just as well as grand, they mark a truly grand ambition, ambition good as well as great." Yes, and why not? Charlotte Brontë used the same term, "honorable ambition," when discussing her attempts to convince her sister Emily to seek publication: "a mind like hers could not be without some latent spark of honorable ambition, and [I] refused to be discouraged in my attempts to fan that spark to flame." We can likewise hear a certain thrill of ambition in Emily Dickinson, including in her poems about being powerless. One paraphrase of those poems seems more accurate than others: I am so little I could destroy you. Dickinson makes us think that tyrants are not ambitious enough, given that they're unable to control or fathom their own psychic horizons.

There is something especially compelling about writers' ambitions, coming as they so often do—in actuality, despite labor and talent—apparently to nothing. Or being believed by the writers (Keats and Dickinson, for instance) to have come to nothing in any public sense. And to turn the question about ambition back upon the writers' creations, where are writers without their characters' ambitions? When it comes to aspiration, there's at least a pinch of Dr. Faustus in every engaging literary character—and I wouldn't exclude Anne of Green Gables.

Huckleberry Finn's "All right, then, I'll go to hell" is as resonant in its own way as Satan's claim (through Milton), "myself am Hell."

Some ambition, depending on its aim, can be a symptom of malignant egotism, the preoccupation of a writer who would succeed at any cost. And yet a lack of ambition can signal timidity—writing small, without courage or discipline. If writing well always takes the form of an experiment, as Theodore Roethke and others have claimed, then we writers may feel like our own specimen tubs. But then, for some, the right to be ambitious signals independence, including those who since childhood heard the phrase "Who died and made you queen?" at the slightest assertion of their human worth.

Ambition has its price, and there is no lack of warnings. Or ridicule. The prospect of public ridicule is even more ominous of late, given the many forums in which writers can be found wanting. No one is safe, especially from reviews on Amazon.com. If you look up Shakespeare's *Macbeth* you'll discover that some readers give it only two stars: "Tacky with very few memorable quotes" and "mediocre plot, mediocre characters." *The Tempest*, too, merited a two-star rating: "Interesting, but just a one-time read."

Ambition can be tainted with arrogance. Even so, arrogance may be a necessary weapon for many writers. Just the same, those accused of being arrogant and who accept the epithet may be anxious to insist that the description involves a matter of degrees. Sherman Alexie responded to an interviewer, "You know, I'm an arrogant guy and sometimes I say things that make me sound like I'm some *very* arrogant guy, but I'm only arrogant. I'm not *very* arrogant. But I play with the big boys."

Edna O'Brien's account of James Joyce's writing of *Ulysses* serves as a wrenching testimony to ambition that should serve to stiffen any writer's spine:

> *Ulysses* took seven years of unbroken labor, twenty thousand hours of work, havoc to brain and body, nerves, agitation, fainting fits, numerous eye complaints—glaucoma, iritis, cataract, crystallized cataract, nebula in the pupil, conjunctivitis, torn retina, blood accumulation, abscesses and one-tenth normal vision. That Joyce has risen above so much misunderstanding is surely a testament to those wounded eyes and the Holy Ghost in that ink bottle.

The aim of ambition is what matters. We have to decide how to fill the concept and what form our relationship to ambition may take. And that's the problem. The act of writing is so dependent on unknowable factors and the momentum forward is so unpredictable that our aims may be continually modified. I don't mean to exaggerate. It's not as if we start out intending to compose a recipe featuring chickpeas and wind up creating a new sort of graphic novel. But the instability of the act, its volatility, and the uncertain likelihood of success, can make predicting the final form an unsettling and sometimes nearly futile venture.

To write imaginatively is to be a student of ambition, our own and that of our characters. In terms of plot, imaginative writing is often about ambition's price. Writers are apt to use ambition as a situational or dramatic device. Some variant of ambition—normally called "desire" or, less dramatically, "motivation"—is at work. Consider the unquenchable will of the governess in Henry James's novella *The Turn of the Screw* or the obsession of a biographer with "The Aspern Papers" in a story of that name, and Miss Tita's determination to destroy those same papers; or consider the grand ambition displayed in the title of Edward Casaubon's unrealized life's work, "The Key to all Mythologies," contrasted with George Eliot's tidy title *Middlemarch* and even more humble subtitle *A Study of Provincial Life*.

§

I recall having lunch a few years ago with a woman who was bitterly criticizing a mutual acquaintance, without specifics. "But what bothers you about her?" I asked, frustrated and wanting to get at the evidence. Voice lowered, as if her words would consign that other woman to damnation forever, my lunch partner said, "She's ambitious."

At another lunch (why do these conversations happen at lunch, and now that I'm reporting them, will anyone ever go to lunch with me again?), another acquaintance praised a woman in the most back-handed way imaginable by claiming she *lacked* ambition: "She's a mediocrity and knows it, but she accepts it and has no qualms about it. I find that quality admirable."

One woman's ambition was disparaged, another woman's purported lack of ambition was praised. I felt sympathy for both of those absent women, defenseless before such judgment. When I recall those lunch conversations I think of a portion of Milan Kundera's *Ignorance* that suggests the most horrible of the vulnerabilities that ambition seeks to overcome:

> For the woman who is dead is a woman with no defenses; she has no more power, she has no more influence; people no longer respect either her wishes or her tastes; the dead woman cannot will anything, cannot aspire to any respect or refute any slander.

What does it mean to "aspire to any respect"? Does it mean to at least attempt to reach toward the limit of one's capacity? And what is ambition, for all its bad reputation, but the antithesis of death, the opposite of the undefended corpse? Ambition seems to prove that, if nothing else, we are in service to a conception of enhanced possibilities. To be ambitious may even mean that we are extraordinarily alive, summoning energy, will, and resonant presence, even while so much that we experience conspires to make all but very few people believe their lives are smaller than they actually are or need to be.

The Closest Work

When I entered grammar school I didn't know the alphabet, and I was slow to learn to read.

In second grade all of us were told we would be awarded a prize if we read ten storybooks. I think I was the only child who didn't receive a prize. One by one, the children sat on the teacher's lap as she gave each a toy. I was too shy to sit on her lap. I reread the tenth book for weeks, never "finishing." To this day I can see the book's illustration of a school bus. It was an ugly book, and it was also a shield.

It's possible, though, that rereading that tenth book was a great help to me. As I steeped myself in those sentences I began to understand what I was reading. Soon, I could hardly stop reading.

Reading and writing, done less than an arm's length away, were accomplished in a small space removed from the more hazardous bewilderments of childhood. Otherwise, outside of the books and the papers on my desk at school, I experienced a sensation of stopping short, halted before a zone that I feared and avoided.

So much of the world was unreliable. It would take me a long time to learn to tell time, a long time to learn to play games on the playground. In many situations I could not understand what other children understood easily. I accepted my own bewilderment as inevitable, and I came to rely on reading and writing as substitutes for all that otherwise I couldn't understand.

I'd already discovered that poems, what little I knew of them, were best for the intense reading I depended on. Poems were like inky apparition, as were poets. I actually thought poets *were* their words. Somehow, I believed poems had materialized after the poets' deaths.

One afternoon a photographer took my picture and remarked, "One of her eyes droops." I was a seven-year-old in my First Communion dress. I was not offended by the photographer's comment but instead felt grateful for his close attention. In the photograph I am seriously trying to be Mary, the Mother of Jesus. Because I forgot my prayer book, I am staring at a blank sheaf of papers at the level of my breastbone. The papers are folded to resemble a book.

By the time it was discovered that I could not see writing on the blackboard at school, not even from the first few rows, that I couldn't read the numerals on the clock on the wall, that I panicked secretly when attempting to recognize the faces of the other children on the playground, I must have been at least nine years old. I had learned to read and write and had promised myself a secret and seemingly impossible ambition—to be a writer—although I never imagined I would be the author of something as extraordinary as an actual book. By then my promise to myself had been conditioned by the fact that I was—like so many others, simply enough, commonly enough—a myopic child.

When the problem with my eyes was discovered and I was at last prescribed glasses, it became obvious to me that by having my extreme near-sightedness corrected I also gained new vulnerabilities. The feelings of other people suddenly became too close. To see clearly meant it was possible to experience more fully others' repugnance or irritation or dismay. There were more colors in people's faces, and the colors took on sharper edges. Yet it was difficult to make any edges appear around myself. When I became a teenager I disliked wearing glasses and tried often, miserably, to go without them—out of vanity and out of the self-protection that young people so often desire.

The sensation of working close to the page, and of struggling to see into vague distances, has influenced my poetry and fiction. My work has also developed in some measure from early experiences in which I had to be careful to speak distinctly and to repeat myself.

I don't remember exactly when my father stopped being able to hear us well. Hearing aids never helped him much, and eventually he gave up trying to wear one. Instead, he taught himself to watch faces intently, to move his lips with our lips as we spoke to him. To be heard by him meant that all of us in our family had to weigh our words. I reduced whatever I needed to say to make repetition easier for myself.

My father doted on me. Even before I became a teenager I felt that he wanted something from me to which he could immediately respond. He wanted words that offered a stubborn quirkiness that answered his own sense of the stubborn quirkiness of life. It was characteristic of him to admire people who worked hard, and yet he was most fond of remarks that reflected an irreverent ebullience, a relief from worry and labor.

At times I would be tired even before I spoke to him, as if it was too much of an effort to repeat myself and to make words interesting enough for him. I was ashamed, because he was so obviously patient with me. I knew, too, that speaking with him could be wonderful—his face reflecting tender surprise. Yet talking with him was also a painful event, as if too much feeling threatened to overcome me. To be listened to with such hope, from someone so eager for laughter, eager for the jarring dislocations of meaning that create laughter: how fortunate I was, and how often his responses made whatever was reluctant to feel within me break open and thaw painfully.

In my early work a tone of voice can be heard that is derived from a training in inflection and repetition that I received by talking with my father, when even the most innocent words bore the potential to baffle, or to meet the undisguised yearning and love in his face.

It is a commonplace to speak of the sensual nature of strong writing. Yet the senses reveal shifts, decay, limitations. The senses live while we live. They may abandon us as they respond to time and trauma.

When I write I gain a recognition of both the boundaries of the senses and my boundaries as a writer, along with the hope of trespassing against those boundaries.

I recognize the note of ambition in the previous sentence. I wouldn't want to deny ambition to any writer, including myself.

Skinned Alive

In one of the most harrowing visual depictions of punished ambition, Titian's painting *The Flaying of Marsyas*, the satyr is skinned alive for his presumption in competing with Apollo—Marsyas's flute against Apollo's lyre. (In many retellings of this Greek myth, divine trickery occurs.) No matter how many times I study the image, its pretty yet cold-blooded Apollo pressing the tip of his knife into the satyr's skin, I can't dismiss the horror. Inevitably I return to stare at the painted body hung upside down, trussed and dressed out like a deer carcass. So many are at work. A little dog laps blood. An old satyr with distended nipples brings a bucket. Apollo fastidiously peels Marsyas's chest. Skin is visible everywhere, bare arms and legs and torsos, and it is the skin of Marsyas's torso that gleams brightest amid that writhing flesh.

The painting was symbolically resonant for the novelist Iris Murdoch in her efforts to pare falsities from her introspective characters. Portions of Titian's painting are included in Tom Phillip's portrait of Murdoch, painted over the course of three years in fifteen sittings. In her wonderful introduction to Murdoch's *The Sea, The Sea*, Mary Kinzie refers to the satyr's agony and the fascination that the painting held for Murdoch as an image of "unspeakable striving," representing "the physical being on the threshold of a spiritual change." As Kinzie puts it, Marsyas "is submitting in terror, yet without struggle, to having the real rind of his symbolically flawed nature sliced away."

Although I admire Kinzie's introduction, I can't be entirely satisfied with an attempt to discover a vision of "the artist ... both defeated and redeemed" in Marsyas's features. Perhaps I have trouble seeing that he is submitting to, and being redeemed by, what has befallen him because I have done the vulgar thing and turned the image upside down, which is easy enough for me to do, given that I downloaded and printed off the image. Of course the painting isn't meant to be viewed upside down, but the satyr being skinned is himself upside down. By inverting the image my perspective is more like his.

When the painting is reversed, the satyr's hoofs almost meet the edge of the canvas. It appears as if he's walking off. His arms, foreshortened, are curved above his head like the dancer Nijinsky's. Stepping away, Marsyas is escaping his tormentors, who now look as if they're hung like fluffy putti in the air. With the image inverted, Marsyas's expression is agonized, his misery undeniable. Is the satyr's suffering, as so many have argued, the artist's—the knife brought to bear, stripping the skin from overbearing ambition? My own explanation may be unsophisticated, but it's one that I experience more acutely each time I look at the reversed image. The satyr has not only lost the competition with a god and is now losing his skin—we know that—but he has lost more. It sounds almost too banal to comment on, but the obvious realization bothers me. For his presumption, Marsyas will never again play the flute. He has lost his music, his gift. He has lost the exalted breath that moves beyond the body.

ξ

Even before writing any notes, I had wanted to call this book *Swallowing the Sea* to suggest and honor the wildly outsized but exhilarating ambition that the act of writing can generate, and as an image of the love of possibility, the love of something astonishing achieved through the imagination.

That was before I even knew of the Chinese folk tale about the five identical brothers, each of whom possessed a miraculous capacity, and one of whom could swallow the sea. That's the brother who gets all his other brothers in trouble. He actually does swallow the sea. Unable to hold the sea any longer, he disgorges it, which leads to the accidental drowning of a boy. When the brother who swallows the sea is about to be executed for causing the death, each of his brothers surreptitiously takes his place in succession and defies the means of execution. The brother with an iron neck can't be beheaded. The brother who stretches like rubber can't be drowned. The brother who only feels pleasantly warm at the stake can't be burned. The brother who continues to breathe anywhere at any time can't be suffocated. Eventually the judge declares that since he can't be destroyed, the brother who swallowed the sea must be an innocent man.

As Iris Murdoch's protagonist in *The Black Prince* says, "Language is a comic form, and makes jokes in its sleep." The writer swallowing the sea defies death with every means. Such a writer's capacities, to the civil authorities, keep changing. Such a writer is an escape artist, even to herself or himself. The sea can't be swallowed forever, not even in that wonderful story from China, but whoever imagines swallowing the sea imagines powerfully.

ξ

When we were children, one of my sisters and I played a game: *Who Can Think the Thought Never Thought Before.* Neither of us, presumably, ever won. One of my problems was that my answers always involved elephants.

ξ

What writer, at least secretly, doesn't harbor some variety of ambition? Every time we take pen to paper or press a series of keys, something absolutely unanticipated can occur. In other words, for many of us, writing is a spectacular form of gambling.

Have You Finished Your One Thousandth Book Yet?

This is unavoidable: We must face connotations. A sense of disconcerting double-dealing attaches to the word *ambition*. According to *Dictionary.com*, ambition is "an earned desire for some type of achievement or distinction, a power, honor, fame, or wealth, and the willingness to strive for its attainment." Note the focus on "earned desire." Good writing is earned and made visible through craft. Writing, after all, is one of the occupations that reveals its practitioners in full light. We stand exposed, with our foibles and fixations and our "earned desires" in view.

Immediately following that definition, however, is a sample sentence that sounds a warning note: "Too much ambition caused him to be disliked by his colleagues."

More often than not, multiple warnings attach to *ambition*. The phrase "vaulting ambition" that "overleaps itself" comes from *Macbeth*, where ambition gallops in the most hideous direction. There's even a word, *ambitionist*, according to *Webster's*, for "one excessively ambitious." The etymology of *ambition* comes from "to go around (for votes)," and thus the term connotes a noxious bid for popularity or the gaining of favor through crafty political means. As an example, *Webster's* presents a particularly disgusting sentence from Trumbull: "Pausanias, ambitioning the sovereignty of Greece, bargains with Xerxes for his daughter in marriage." Or we might cite the chorus of Marlowe's *Doctor Faustus*:

> Faustus is gone: regard his hellish fall,
> Whose fiendful fortune may exhort the wise
> Only to wonder at unlawful things
> Whose deepness doth entice such forward wits
> To practice more than heavenly power permits.

ξ

Conventional evidence of writerly ambition turns up as prolific output and work habits of incredible steadiness measured in hours or pages, and stated desires calculated in terms of outrageousness.

Who can avoid thinking of ambition as measureable achievement? In *My Unwritten Books*, George Steiner recounts a line that he heard J. Robert Oppenheimer "fling" toward "a junior physicist": "You are so young and *already* you have done so little." Jorge Luis Borges, one of the most self-deprecating of writers, also made quantity a measure of accomplishment—in terms of committing errors: "I think I have committed not all the possible mistakes—because mistakes are innumerable—but many of them." Then too, there is the abundant productivity of canonical writers, such as Shakespeare (despite his middle-age retirement), Milton (blind, dictating to his daughters), and Homer (whether he existed as one person or several). Closer to our own time, there's Prentiss Ingraham (1843–1904), who boasted of having written roughly thirty-five thousand words in a single day, composing in his lifetime a total of more than six hundred books. He's outdone by one of our contemporaries, the Judaism scholar Jacob Neusner, who has an oeuvre of roughly a thousand books.

Sometimes, in lieu of a thousand books, an attitude will do. The *New York Times* obituary of Norman Mailer noted that "[h]e was the most transparently ambitious writer of his era, seeing himself in competition not just with his contemporaries but with the likes of Tolstoy and Dostoevsky." Mailer spurred himself on to re-imagine no less than the life of Jesus in *The Gospel According to the Son* and to narrate the life of Hitler through the voice of a devil in *The Castle in the Forest*, two feats that testify to the span and scale of his ambitions.

Of course writers have their forebears to measure themselves against. Decades ago, Donald Hall called for heightened aspirations in striking terms: "If our goal in life is to remain content, *no* great ambition is sensible ... If our goal is to write poetry, the only way we are likely to be *any* good is to try to be as great as the best."

Franz Kafka clung to writing with desperation and a form of torturous ambition. In 1913, "out of boredom and despair," he had his cards read by a Russian woman. He stated to Felix Weltsch in a letter that the cards, while not to be taken "literally," may impose "clarity into what is otherwise a confused and opaque realm." The cards gave him a reading unlike anyone else's in the room. "[T]here constantly revolved around me 'Troubles,' 'Wealth,' and 'Ambition,' the sole abstractions, outside of 'Love,' known to the cards." In 1922 Kafka wrote to Max Brod of his pained conviction: "The existence of the writer is truly dependent upon his desk and if he wants to keep madness at bay he must never go far from his desk, he must hold on to it with his teeth."

Like Kafka, Balzac refused to be torn from his writing. Purportedly he wrote fifteen to eighteen hours each day, generally while on his feet and stomaching endless cups of coffee, over his lifetime producing roughly one hundred full-scale novels and plays. Less well known: Balzac is the author of the phrase "A flow of words is a sure sign of duplicity."

At the same time, we may want our writers to display an Olympian resistance to measuring ambition by any means. Who is the best candidate for that honor? Off the top of many heads the answer would be Emily Dickinson. It's hard to imagine Dickinson, at least past her early years, in a parlor balancing both a glass of sherry and a posse of admirers. Recall her famous line, "Publication is the Auction / of the Mind of Man—." Although the number of her individual poems published while she lived can be disputed, it's generally recognized to be under a dozen. Sensitive to the point of view of the powerless and irreconcilable to settled patterns of belief, she wrote over a thousand poems but published no book in her lifetime. Imagine what we would tell Dickinson if we could visit her in the past, and if she let us into her house: Your words will be emblazoned on a coffee cup, your face on a stamp, your dress on a doll named after you. Publicity *is* the auction of your mind, believe me.

Then again, who could actually think they've bought Dickinson's mind, no matter how often the auction occurs? As if Dickinson's mind could be a shapely bauble. "The Brain—is—wider than the Sky—," she wrote. No one yet has auctioned the sky ... entirely.

ξ

Mary Shelley's psychologically complex author's introduction to *Frankenstein* is one of the most compelling assertions of writerly ambition, given that Shelley, then only a teenager, was competing with masters of her era (with one of whom she had eloped) as well as cultural resistance to female achievement. Bored by gloomy weather, anxious to prove her worth before the luminaries around her, she realized her desires.

> "We will each write a ghost story," said Lord Byron, and his proposition was acceded to. There were four of us. The noble author began a tale, a fragment of which he printed at the end of his poem "Mazeppa." Shelley, more apt to embody ideas and sentiments in the radiance of brilliant imagery and in the music of the most melodious verse that adorns our language than to invent the machinery of a story, commenced one founded on the experiences of his early life. Poor Polidori had some terrible idea about a skull-headed lady who was so punished for peeping through a key-hole—what to see I forget: something very shocking and wrong of course; but when she was reduced to a worse condition than the renowned Tom of Coventry, he did not know what to do with her and was obliged to dispatch her to the tomb of the Capulets, the only place for which she was fitted. The illustrious poets also, an-

noyed by the platitude of prose, speedily relinquished their uncongenial task.

I busied myself *to think of a story*—a story to rival those which had excited us to this task.

Mary Shelley was determined to avoid becoming Polidori's lady peering through the keyhole. If she peered (and the monster she creates is often a voyeur), she resisted being drawn by her rivals to the tomb of the Capulets. And what is her monster but an embodiment of unquenchable, unappeasable striving that can't be destroyed by any hands but his own? *Frankenstein* is a warning not only about unlimited ambition, about unintended consequences, about scientific adventurism, about parental abandonment, about a daughter's fear of being monstrous, but also about the dread of failing to fulfill a dare that begins with a writing prompt. This is a story, in some ways, about being a writer. Dr. Frankenstein, like a writer, excavates the dead (the past, memory, literary legacy); connects and rearranges the parts; conducts further experiments; tightens the screws; and waits for a miracle. Despite his labors he deems himself a failure. When his creation doesn't live up to his expectations he abandons it. Any writer knows: he should have revised.

Fear of failing to meet one's own expectations, let alone anyone else's, or fear of mortality and decay and oblivion—those fears propel writers. Think of the Greek poet Constantine Cavafy, that scourger of regret and hesitancy, that laureate of nostalgia. Or recall Proust's essences decanted with a slow but obsessive urgency. Or sickly Robert Louis Stevenson in *A Child's Garden of Verses* putting to bed an ill child who imagines his way into other lands:

> I was the giant great and still
> That sits upon the pillow-hill,
> And sees before him, dale and plain,
> The pleasant land of counterpane.

Or Keats, struggling with the tuberculosis that doomed him, and who is heartbreaking in "To Autumn" in his disguised desires "To bend with apples," and "fill all fruit with ripeness to the core." His ambition is made into exalted and struggled-for dignity in "When I Have Fears That I May Cease to Be":

> When I have fears that I may cease to be
>   Before my pen has gleaned my teeming brain,
> Before high-piled books, in charact'ry,
>   Hold like rich garners the full ripened grain;
> When I behold, upon the night's starr'd face,
>   Huge cloudy symbols of a high romance,
> And think that I may never live to trace
>   Their shadows, with the magic hand of chance;
> And when I feel, fair creature of an hour!
>   That I shall never look upon thee more,
> Never have relish in the faery power
>   Of unreflecting love;—then on the shore
> Of the wide world I stand alone, and think
> Till love and fame to nothingness do sink.

Less well known is "Floating Bridges" by Federico García Lorca, who would die by Franco's firing squad in 1936:

> Oh garden of white
> theories! garden
> of all I am not, all
> I could & should have been!

Paying Tribute to the Unappeasable

Once at a retirement home I watched a woman clutching a filthy stuffed animal—Big Bird—and talking into its frothy yellow face with such swelling intensity that everyone around her was half in tears. A man I knew tried to fight loneliness by going to auctions to make friends but acquired only antiques instead, until his garage filled and he began stuffing everything under his porch.

There's a loneliness that even social interaction doesn't alleviate. I confess to being so lonely for a year that nothing would help, not even helping others (the usual antidote), not even meeting new people. At about that time, I discovered a second-hand copy of Rachel Ingalls's *Mrs. Caliban*.

The cover of the Laurel edition of the novel shows a drawing of an eye-less, nipple-less, naked orange woman rising across from a green man with brown spots, yellow eyes, and webbed feet. Under the monster's arm is the seal of approval from the British Book Marketing Council: ONE OF THE 20 GREATEST AMERICAN POST-WORLD WAR II NOVELS!

Mrs. Caliban is an exquisite little book that pays tribute to the unappeasable. And the novel tells us as much about ambition as it does about a particularly desperate form of adultery.

The plot of Ingalls's 1983 novel is simple: A lonely Californian in grief over a miscarriage and the death of her young son, and numb from her husband's adulteries, begins hearing radio messages addressed only to her. When a monster, escaped from an experimental lab, invades her kitchen, the encounter between woman and monster is brilliantly rendered as a collision between mundane and fantastic acts:

> She came back into the kitchen fast, to make sure that she caught the toasting cheese in time. And she was halfway across the checked linoleum floor of her nice safe kitchen,

when the screen door opened and a gigantic six-foot-seven-inch frog-like creature shouldered its way into the house and stood stock-still in front of her, crouching slightly, and staring straight at her face.

She stopped before she knew she had stopped, and looked, without realizing she was taking anything in. She was as surprised and shocked as if she had heard an explosion and seen her own shattered legs go flying across the floor. There was a space between him and the space where she was standing; it was like a gap in time. She saw how slowly everything was happening.

What can the woman do but offer the monster celery and have sex with him in every room of the house?

Like the heroine of L. Frank Baum's *The Wonderful Wizard of Oz*, Ingall's protaganist is named Dorothy. She, too, finds hope in the color green, but her dog, a Toto-like companion, has died before the action of the novel begins; one of her friends is truly made of tin; and she has been lied to longer than Baum's little Dorothy was ever lied to by her wizard.

The book is a revenge fantasy. Despite neurological evidence indicating that acts of revenge light up pleasure centers in the brain, revenge in *Mrs. Caliban* doesn't feel particularly good. Yet Dorothy does escape her predatory sister-in-law and wipes her life clean of principal betrayals.

The monster is a fallible replacement for all Dorothy has lost. He's curious, helpful, incapable of lying, and as confused by her world as she is. Whether or not Dorothy has invented her green beast, her loss of him at the end of the novel means loneliness is renewed and duplicities reverberate:

She drove down in the evenings to the beach. Sometimes by

moonlight and sometimes only by starlight, she stared at the line where the water ran over the sand. He never came. She got out of the car and walked up and down the beach, hour after hour. The water ran over the sand, one wave covering another like the knitting of threads, like the begetting of revenges, betrayals, memories, regrets. And always it made a musical, murmuring sound, a language as definite as speech.

But he never came.

The experience of reading *Mrs. Caliban* is so deeply interior as to feel almost shameful, like the passivity endured in a nightmare when the murderer appears at the top of the stairs and you can't run but find your feet planted on the lowest step. At points the narrative could handily illustrate *Freud for Dummies*. An umbrella, particularly a retractable one, is not just an umbrella. Then, too, in this novel we are allowed to entertain a guided daydream, cloud-propelled, on the other side of the nightmare. The novel's despair and hopelessness are shot through with an eerie pleasure that isn't exactly pornographic but is stirringly evocative of secret angers and even more secret resentments.

There's elevator fiction and there's escalator fiction. The latter takes its time and you see more along the way. By contrast, *Mrs. Caliban* is high-rise elevator fiction. Before you know it, you've arrived at the top floor and the ride is over. Although vaguely comical, the novel is capable of re-igniting a sensation close to heartbreak—the kind most of us have armored ourselves against.

The novel is ambitiously constructed, merging elements from romance, science fiction, metaphysical revenge tragedies, and fairy tales, meanwhile making sure its heroine scours the earth of her every enemy. Despite the Shakespearean reference in the title, most prominent are Ingalls's debts to fairy tales, and thus the novel is propelled by a potent force. Among those English-language verbal arts not claiming to be Shakespearean or Miltonic or Dickinsonian, and not inspired by anyone's god, mystic, or saint, the most inexhaustible are nursery rhymes, folk songs, and fairy tales. There's little in literature that doesn't pale before their economy and durabilty. Almost any nursery rhyme or fairy tale can be tugged for any occasion or mood or even debility—including the writer's anguish:

> *Oh dear, what can the matter be?* That's our subject.
> *Little Blue Readers:* You can blow your own horn, but they're still fast asleep.

Gleeful malice runs through nursery rhymes and fairy tales. Most of them are anonymous memory bundles, born in oral tradition, seldom betraying the identity of an original individual voice of invention. As such, we don't think of them as "ambitious," even though they straddle cultures and colonize the mind, even though they probe the most sinister instincts. That is, they're not ambitious in the generally understood sense, for ambition is a word we experience as most often connected to individual actors. Faust is not, nor ever was, a committee. In order for Ingalls's novel to stake its claims to ambition the novel has to wear personal idiosyncrasies, which it certainly does. But by drawing from the deep well of the fairy tale, Ingalls makes her betrayed housewife a more encompassing and more powerful force of destruction.

To flirt with literary failure presumes ambition: avoiding the sure thing, responding to an ideal vision that may keep disappearing as we approach, like the mirage that idealizations tend to be. The endeavor is exciting, unless we persecute ourselves with the imperative of the grandmother in Isaac Babel's story (titled by the grandmother's words to her grandson) "*You must know everything.*"

FAILURE

You Flirt with Failure but You Marry Ambition

"I USUALLY SOLVE PROBLEMS BY LETTING THEM DEVOUR ME." —FRANZ KAFKA

For elegance, longevity, and the ability to crop up in nearly any rhetorical situation until you could groan, one of the most successful lines in literature is Tolstoy's "Happy families are all alike; every unhappy family is unhappy in its own way." And the statement is not even—as everybody likes to point out—true. All successes aren't alike, but failures are truly deeply different.

Failure: the shock of irreversible disease, exile, a city destroyed, an ill mind untreatable, death. Success isn't the opposite of failure. The miracle is.

But miracles tend to stun us or incite disbelief. Failure is where we are forced to confront ourselves. Consider best-selling memoirs: *Look at my failures, please.* Best-selling fiction: *Look at my protagonist's enemies, who are destined to fail like your enemies will fail, believe me.*

Samuel Beckett's words from *Worstward Ho,* adopted as the watchwords of the popular website *Failbetter.com* and now proving ubiquitous, no doubt resonate with anyone who has ever attempted to make art: "Ever tried. Ever failed. No matter. Try again. Fail again. Fail better." The novelist John Banville, quoting Beckett, observed in *Tin House,* "It's all we can do. Everybody fails. The acknowledgment of that failure is very important. Perfection is not of this world. It's the quality of the failure that counts."

Love of failure ... courting failure ... "the quality of the failure."

All happy writers aren't alike. But more unhappiness comes from inflated expectations of approval and understanding than from inflated visions.

Two causes of literary failure come to mind: perfectionism and hysterical impatience. The adjustocrats of perfection say, *Why did you use so much rat poison, Madame Bovary?* The adjustocrats of impatience say, *Why can't your art be like mushrooms: ready overnight, heads crowning, apparitions-to-go?*

A third cause of failure: the desire to be admired when that wish conflicts with one's literary instincts.

A fourth cause: your publisher. Muriel Spark, in *Loitering with Intent*, says it best: "The traditional paranoia of authors is as nothing compared to the inalienable schizophrenia of publishers."

Failure has its accomplices, including addiction to drugs or alcohol; ill health, whether mental or physical or both; misplaced ambition; early success that throws a writer off stride or too readily mummifies a reputation; repeated rejections; emotional "paralysis," particularly that which is fueled by anticipating the reactions of reviewers (those bad fairies at the christening of any book); ongoing emotional exhaustion caused by trying to both write and make a living; and so on. Then there is always the problem of time. As Maxwell Perkins told James Jones, "Time is the enemy of us all, and especially of the writer."

Some variant of nearly every affliction listed above was suffered by F. Scott Fitzgerald. In his essay "The Crack-Up," first published in 1936 in *Esquire*, he anatomizes his loss of "vitality," and in an extension of that essay, "Handle with Care," he returns to his "cracked plate" analogy to describe his terrible breakdown and depression. Using other metaphors, he complains of "a feeling that I was standing at twilight on a deserted range, with an empty rifle in my hands and the target down." His deliberations make for sobering reading.

Like anyone else, writers face temptations, but unlike many professions, writing involves making sure one's inventions—in terms of plot—encounter failure. No matter how miserably we're doing ourselves, or how kind our natures, we have to make sure that we give our creations a hard time. Ironically, if we're too soft on our characters they won't survive. In much of Western canonical literature, conventional success is overturned or shadowed with ambiguity to a point that's almost fetishistic. Characters that court unintended consequences and fail wildly and broadly may qualify for the subject of great art. Seldom, in the plots of superior literature, will you hear many remedies:

> *Why don't you marry Brett, now that her little matador is out of the way?*
> *Couldn't paradise be, you know, not lost, just misplaced?*

There's an outlandish freedom demanded by writers and afforded their characters: freedom to fail. Freedom to represent and re-represent failure. In Evelyn Waugh's *Vile Bodies*, the failure of a greeting in terms of social etiquette is a triumph in terms of literary etiquette, as Lottie Crump declares, "Bless you, I knew you before you were born. How's your father? Not dead, is he?"

It's inevitable, then, that in considering ambition, writers must think about ambition's nemesis: failure—both the failures that they must heartlessly visit upon their characters in pursuit of successful dramatic action and the failures that they can call their own.

Rejection: Haven't We Met Before?

Borges makes a marvelous distinction: "[O]ne reads what one likes— yet one writes not what one would like to write, but what one is able to write." At times, writers have to reject certain writing projects as unsuitable to their talents. More often, publishers reject certain writing projects as unsuitable for their list.

> *I find your . . . contradictory.*
> *I find your . . . painfully inadequate.*

I find your . . . avoidable.

You've done a lot with your . . ., but it's marred by the Bluebeard-like obsessions hanging in the rafters of your inane prose.

ξ

The duck goes to the famous literary doctor's office with an envelope and says, *Can you help me? I'm so weak I can't open my bill.*

Sorry. I can't help you. You'll die in sixty days.

What do you know? You're a quack.

And you're a solipsist.

ξ

In Brian Morton's novel *Starting Out in the Evening,* the aged writer Leonard Schiller notes, "When you've been a writer for a long time, you develop an uncanny sensitivity to barely perceptible verbal signals of rejection." (The film by the same title is the only film I know of that captures the single-minded devotion to writing, the despair when ambition meets bodily decay, and the dreadful suspense of wondering if a very sick man will touch the keys of his typewriter again.) The acute rejection that Morton writes about comes at writers from nearly every direction, perhaps most often from the writer's own self. Not only can we not please everybody, including, too often, ourselves, we can't please even a significant minority of people, not most of us, even some of the best of us. Rejection can occur posthumously and in odd ways. Several years ago a student wrote a note on a final exam I gave on the modernist poets. The note read: "Wallace Stevens, go to hell."

There may be even after-the-fact rejections by our friends. Writers tend to sign books and thereby supply evidence of their hope that what's between the covers will be treasured. This scenario may be familiar to you. You open a book that looks interesting in a used book store. Inside the front cover is the author's autograph and three lines of affectionate endearments and a little ink drawing that the author spent some time on, evidently meaning to amuse and charm. And there you stand, the book, ready to be sold, in your hands. You are an accidental voyeur.

ξ

By the time I was eleven I often rode my bike the three miles to Maple Rapids to visit the public library. Sadly, that library has since disappeared. The building used to be someone's exceptionally tiny house, and the books on the shelves never looked new. That was part of those books' appeal. Their covers, some as brown as walnut shells, were dusty, their spines raggedy, with threads coming loose. Cracked open, the books gave off the sweetly decaying smell of old leaves. In Alan Hollinghurst's novel *The Stranger's Child*, a small precise action brought back so much tactile memory of that library that I had to put the book down: "He trailed his fingers along the spines of the books in the bookcase as he passed, producing a low steady ripple."

The librarian kept trying to herd me into the children's section, just around the alcove. I preferred the adult section.

In *When I Was a Child I Read Books*, Marilynne Robinson writes, "I remember once, as a child, walking into a library, looking around at the books, and thinking, I could do that."

My own experience differed. Although I started a little newspaper for home-only distribution called The Grand Prix (I'd read those words but had never heard them said, and so you can imagine how I pronounced them), and although I hoped that I might someday write something that could end up in an actual newspaper distributed beyond my own home, writing an actual book didn't appear possible. I revered books so much it's a wonder I ever published anything.

By sixth grade, I was reading *Macbeth* aloud in the darkened cellar of our house and, to conjure what I thought was the right atmosphere, waving a butcher knife by the cider barrel.

In college when I began sending my writing out to literary journals I expected rejection. That way, rejection would never surprise me. Even then I couldn't imagine I would ever see a book of my own published. No doubt, in my case, such low expectations of possibility had something to do with my gender. There's a sentence in Alice Munro's short story "Haven" that sums up the situation: "Devotion to anything, if you were female, could make you ridiculous."

To be fair, I don't remember any of the boys I grew up with expressing their ambitions either. Maybe they would have been considered ridiculous too. And yet how I managed was by devotion, by moving ahead with the difficult joy of writing, by hope more than faith, by saving my ambition for the writing itself, where ambition flourishes in the form of imaginative freedom. Besides which, I was born into a family with a sense of humor, which meant the ridiculous had its appeal.

ξ

Interviewer: What is your relationship to your readers?

Writer A: *They do not exist, fortunately.*
Writer B: *They exist, unfortunately.*
Writer C: *My readers are to me as the mouse trap is to the giant Norwegian rat—an inconvenience to be overcome.*

Given that readers cast the final vote on rejection, the writer's relationship to them can be characterized by strain. Julian Barnes in

Nothing to be Frightened Of turns the tables:

> I may be dead by the time you are reading this sentence. In which case, any complaints about the book will not be answered. On the other hand, we may both be alive now … but you could die before me. Had you thought of that?

As Barnes's comically defensive maneuver suggests, readers ask much of authors. Readers who are authors tend to ask at least as much. Jonathan Franzen in his introduction to Paula Fox's *Desperate Characters* presents a particularly candid portrayal of author-to-author expectations and the inverse of rejection—a resonant acceptance that slap-cuffs a few famous authors along the way:

> The first time I read *Desperate Characters*, in 1991, I fell in love with it. It seemed to me obviously superior to any novel by Fox's contemporaries John Updike, Philip Roth, and Saul Bellow. It seemed inarguably great. And because I'd recognized my own troubled marriage in the Bentwoods', and because the novel had appeared to suggest that the fear of pain is more destructive than pain itself, and because I wanted very much to believe this, I reread it almost immediately. I hoped that the book, on a second reading, might actually tell me how to live.
>
> It did no such thing. It became instead, more mysterious—became less of a lesson and more of an experience.

Great expectations are what practicing writers may load upon other practicing writers. Then again, writers who don't write may find themselves practicing envy (that advance warning system for writers; if you envy it, you should attempt it).

Most writers who are successful are assumed to have failed in some quarters. I was in the room when one of the most highly regarded writers of the past century was approached by a stranger who, with a smile, recited a litany of all the prizes the writer had failed to win. On another night, a revered poet who at the time was desperately ill listened to a college student say to him, "It must be hard to be you and not be famous."

After witnessing such ordeals, I think of Flannery O'Connor and her admirably caustic sense of humor. She possessed a healthy degree of self-worth as a writer, and a no-nonsense approach to what diminished her. After receiving correspondence from an editor to whom she had submitted her first novel manuscript she complained: "The letter is addressed to a slightly dim-witted Camp Fire Girl, and I cannot look with composure on getting a lifetime of others like them." At a later date when she asked her publisher to mail out complimentary copies of one of her books, she included the observation, "My nine copies have to go to a set of relatives who are waiting anxiously to condemn the book until they get a free copy."

The irony is that for many of us, even success comes with little hooves ready to drum upon moments when we believe our work is being appreciated. Once during a reading while I was honored to be reciting my poems, a man in the audience squealed like a pig. I would have been more bothered, but at the time I thought it was machinery malfunctioning.

Given the likely prospect of rejection in any writer's life, it strikes me as bizarre that some writers claim to maintain files of rejection letters. Keeping those letters, or, more likely, mass-produced notes, is like hoarding splinters plucked from your palm, and then inserting them into your own eye.

Yet there's at least one well-known story of a rejection letter that fanned ambition. In her account of how she and her sisters sought to be published, Charlotte Brontë avowed that failure in the early stages couldn't dampen their desire: "Ill-success failed to crush us:

the mere effort to succeed had given a wonderful zest to experience; it must be pursued." Yet while publishers eventually accepted her sisters' novels, Charlotte's own manuscript was roundly rejected. The work "found acceptance nowhere, nor any acknowledgment of merit, so that something like the chill of despair began to invade [my] heart." When at last she received a rejection letter from a publisher who took her work seriously and carefully explained why her novel was rejected, she returned to writing with new conviction: "This very refusal cheered the author better than a vulgarly expressed acceptance would have done." She had been working on another novel. Within three weeks of receiving that first thoughtful rejection she sent her new manuscript to the one and only publisher who had responded with sympathy to her earlier effort. This publisher was not only sympathetic but expeditious. *Jane Eyre* appeared before either of her sisters' books, *Wuthering Heights* and *Agnes Grey*.

Happily enough, there are accounts of rejections that only masquerade as failures: failures controlled, failures redeemed, failures made into art.

It's not easy to experiment with failure. "The art of losing isn't hard to master," Elizabeth Bishop insisted. But she was being ironic. The rejection narrated in writing, the rejection fully and precisely rendered, touched, apprehended, becomes something close to a masterwork.

Turning Failure Inside Out

There are two narratives of failure that I find particularly heartening. One comes from fiction, the other from poetry.

Alberto Moravia's *Conjugal Love* (1949) is narrated by an ambitious man who derides his ability to narrate, declaring himself a failure. The plot is simple. Deciding to compose a novel, Silvio goes off with his wife to Tuscany and conceives a pact: They'll suspend sexual relations while he writes, to preserve his "aggression" for the page. The post-writing state he later describes may be familiar:

> All that remained after those ardent morning hours [of writing] was the residue, the ashes and cinders of a glorious blaze; and until the new blaze was kindled, next morning, I was left strangely inert and detached, filled with an almost morbid sense of well-being, indifferent to everything … I was, for the first time in my life, outside myself, in an independent, perfect world all made up of harmony and certainty. This state made me selfish …

As soon as Silvio types and then reads the entire manuscript he discovers he had misjudged his work. In *Conjugal Love* the crash comes in the fourteenth chapter with his precise calibrations of his novel's deficiency in terms of "plasticity," "psychological truth," "feeling," and "plot":

> The book [is that] of a dilettante, of a person who, though endowed with intelligence, culture and taste, is completely lacking in creative powers. The book fails to reveal anything fresh, or any fresh turn of sensibility. It is a book founded upon other books, it is second or third rate in quality, it is a hot-house product.

To make matters worse, on the very night that Silvio recognizes his failure as a novelist he discovers his failure as a husband. He is being cuckolded by his barber.

Surprisingly, despite her tryst with the barber, Silvio's wife restores her husband's faith in himself, their marriage, and his own talent for novel-writing by advising patience and a return to the manuscript. Silvio's self-reflection concludes the novel: "'It'll take a long time,' I said softly, finishing my thought aloud."

The novel that we have been reading is Silvio's successful account of his failures in work and love. At last he knows the instinctive little demon who rules his heart. His narcissistic wish for a wholly inspired piece of writing must capitulate to realistic expectations, the cultivation of wisdom, and—if he is ever to achieve anything close to his ambitions—concentrated discipline. We have seen Silvio underestimate his wife from the start, but the novel itself becomes proof of her good sense.

In his novel, then, Moravia works from the inside out, inside failure, and his unreliable narrator, initially dense, arrogant, superior-sounding, is revealed as flawed but ultimately triumphant. By writing a record of failure, Moravia (like Silvio) writes into being his ambitious success. So what do we have? An exploration of will, discipline and inspiration, cerebral knowledge and bodily recognition, all premised on the storyteller being a failure as a storyteller.

Incapacity Attended to Becomes Capacity—for the Admirer

Another narrative of failure that strikes me as heartening is presented implicitly in Elizabeth Bishop's "Poem" (from *Geography III*), which takes as its ostensible subject a great-uncle's undervalued, unsophisticated painting that has been passed on thoughtlessly, confined to attics, hardly meriting an anecdote. Like the dollar bill to which it's compared in shape and tint, the painting becomes currency, a representation of value that can be transformed into something else.

Bishop sets before us a whimsical catalogue of the painting's inadequacies, but turns the painting's failure as visual art into a moment of recognition; "how live, how touching in detail / —the little that we get for free." The painting's very fragility and near anonymity, its inability to earn a dollar, becomes part of the painting's most valued identity.

What Bishop finds through the painting's failure as visual art is an opportunity to contemplate worth, redemption, and conversion, and to display tenderness. The trope of the poem is toward ever greater accuracy. Bishop composes the illusion of a faithful mimesis through minute discriminations about the canvas's unstable surface: flyspeck or fly, steeple or hair from the paintbrush. We do not pity the poem's achieved representation, even as we may feel pity for a version of the painter's implied story that is linked to the human condition of failure. Herself a painter, Bishop accorded to her visual art an ease and casualness that she never allowed her poetry in the process of making it, given her tendency for extreme revision. Yet her poems were crafted to bear a tone of spontaneity, with the illusion of off-hand self-corrections, seemingly impromptu discoveries, and felicitous imperfections common to conversation. In "Poem" the urge to describe the painting's quaintness generates sympathy toward a valiant comic process that flounders until the painting is given attention and, simultaneously, a second life in poetry. It is the quality of focused observation that redeems the failure. In contrast to Moravia in *Conjugal Love*, Bishop works here from the outside in, as attention transforms. Perceived failure of visual artistry becomes an occasion for an ambitious rendering in poetry.

"I Didn't Sleep with Him for His Prose Style"

Why do certain writers compel us to return to them? Muriel Spark compels, not least of all because she is capable of comically dismissing the consequences of failure and of narrating the way art can lure us beyond conventional views of failure. Two books by Muriel Spark illuminate the issue. One is a book about an ambitious failure, the other about an ambitious success.

My fascination with Spark began a few years ago with a character's ruminations:

> "I could kill him," thought Rowland. "But would that be enough?"

There it was, a guiltless and salty defense of instinct and discrimination. The sentiment—"I could kill him … But would that be enough?"—can be clocked like a joke.

Does it help to know that the person considering murder is a failed writer envious of another writer? The line is from Muriel Spark's *The Finishing School* (2004), which focuses on a blocked novelist intent on finishing off his seventeen-year-old student's writing talent—and the student himself. The novel not only excoriates the envious. It proves to be a cautionary tale for anyone who grows dependent on and enjoys being envied.

The Finishing School is the last in a long line of the Scottish author's novels that have been described in some quarters as "glittering." Yes, and reading her is like walking barefoot on a floor on which a glass recently shattered. Glitteringly. But then again, we've had some wine and there's a handsome doctor in attendance, and it's a party. You're single, as is the doctor, and, look, he trembles holding your foot. It's that kind of party.

The Prime of Miss Jean Brodie has overshadowed Spark's other books, many of which are at least as satisfying, in a vinegary sort of way. Among the best is *Loitering with Intent* (1981), which serves as an inversion of *The Finishing School*. Where *The Finishing School* tracks how writers can be "finished," failing in the worst way, *Loitering with Intent* charts a young novelist's steady self-assurance and entirely satisfying ambition. The novel is metafictional to the core, as life turns into fiction and fiction into life, and the art of the reversal gets one workout after another. The protagonist, Fleur Talbot, is not simply recording events as she writes. Her unfinished novel actually makes events happen. If Freud was right about unconscious wishes and literature, Spark must have wanted the power to turn the world into a novel.

Fleur's poverty, the shabbiness of her room, and her romantic problems can't depress her because she's doing that astonishing thing: writing a novel. Writing, she says, is "like being in love and better." When told that "Pride goes before a fall" she responds with reflections on her writing: "In fact if I had pride it was vocational in nature; I couldn't help it, and I've never found it necessarily precedes falls."

Fleur collects impressions meticulously, which is one of the secrets of her success: "But you must understand that everything happens to an artist; time is always redeemed, nothing is lost and wonders never cease."

Spark herself collected prodigious amounts of evidence from her own life from the 1940s onward. The National Library of Scotland counts her archive as one of their most extensive, including among its vast holdings her 1950 library card from the British Library, school certificates, correspondence from Elizabeth Taylor, diaries, photos, betting forms on her horse, and her checkbooks.

Like someone taking Henry James's injunction to heart, nothing is lost on Spark's character Fleur. What she calls the "beautifully awful"—the arch, the artificial, the repressive, the pompous, "the swinish"—all are grist for her novel. "I was aware of a *daemon* inside me that rejoiced in seeing people as they were, and not only that, but more than ever as they were, and more, and more."

As newly hired secretary to the freakish Autobiographical Association, Fleur edits and revises clients' memoirs, discovering that each encapsulates the worst temptations of the genre: "one of them was nostalgia, another was paranoia, a third was a transparent craving on the part of the author to appear likeable." Her reflections on clients' entries accompany reflections on her own craft.

Loitering with Intent doesn't give us a tract on writing, *tract* being the sort of word Spark despised. While some of Fleur's claims about novel-writing are delivered with irony, a good many echo Spark's own suppositions as expressed in interviews and apparently melded with the author's practices. Fleur's major suggestion is her least negotiable: Savor the weird. She also advocates highlighting the "contradictory" in forming characters. As Fleur tells us, "Since the story of my own life is just as much constituted of the secrets of my craft as it is of other events, I might as well remark here that to make a character ring true its needs must be in some way contradictory, somewhere a paradox."

Characters can be identified through repetitive habits, like Maisie in *Loitering with Intent,* who is repeatedly tagged by the way she holds her purse like the reins of the horse that crippled her in a riding accident. Fleur advises that omissions are useful: ". . . complete frankness is not a quality that favors art." And most indicative of a Spark novel: Bend the future and slide it into the present. Often in a Spark novel we know in advance when characters will die, in days, weeks, or years, and this puts the reader in an incredible position. As her characters flounder, we see the futility of action cast against an immutable future. We know when and how the ultimate earthly failure will await these characters, and our knowledge is concrete in a way it can never be in life.

Like Barbara Pym, Anita Brookner, and Ivy Compton-Burnett, Spark labors in the tradition of obsessive repetition. She often presents a narrative involving a crime, particularly blackmail, and then works up aphorism-filled sequences that sting the credulous flunky and the deluded fanatic, the hypocrite whose lack of self-reflection annoys, and the busybody who keeps reappearing like a minor at a beer tent. The character who is legally obligated to and controlled by another—enmeshed, with little recourse—recurs often in her work, and seems by all accounts to reflect Spark's experience of the marriage she fled as a young woman.

Martyrs—those specialists in despair, reduced hopes, and extinguished desire—are her forte, to debunk and deflate. Spark has a great deal of fun with her evil martyr-like characters and their cast of slavish flunkies. Here's a character's entrance in *Loitering with Intent:* "In came the self-evident and luminous little mess." A former lover is compared to a "lard-laden Cornish pasty." In *The Comforters*, Spark's first novel, she takes a bit of revenge-by-description on the deplorable martyr-emulator Georgina Hogg by recalling little boys' fascination with that character's chest. One boy "declared that under her blouse she kept pairs of vegetable marrows, of infant whales, St. Paul's Cathedrals, goldfish bowls." Another boy notices her undergarments: "one of them gave her four breasts, another gave her the life-jacket look ... in ... dangerous sea-faring picture books." A mixture of sternness, wit and mischief, and the courage to hold out and champion eccentricity serve to oppose the martyr.

In many of Spark's novels, including *Loitering with Intent* and *The Finishing School*, the principal discovery amounts to what Kinsley Amis's title character in *Lucky Jim* entertains, in the roughest paraphrase: What's nice is nice. Except that Spark is more often focused on the negative side of the equation: "The not nice aren't nice. Don't trust them. Enjoy them."

Despite all the trouble Spark gets her characters into, she blesses Fleur Talbot in *Loitering with Intent* with ultimate immunity to failure. Failure is almost beside the point for someone so fiercely willful. Consider how Fleur answers a madly annoying and foolish detractor who happens to be the wife of the man in question: "I didn't sleep with him for his prose style." Expect no piety from Fleur. She reflects with wholesome candor on the expectations of readers:

> I wasn't writing poetry and prose so that the reader would think me a nice person, but in order that my sets of words should convey ideas of truth and wonder, as indeed they did

to myself as I was composing them. I see no reason to keep silent about my enjoyment of the sound of my own voice as I work.

It's a rare event in literary fiction when a young artist is depicted as retaining unalloyed faith in her own art and its potentials for pleasure. As Fleur exclaims, "What a wonderful thing it was to be a woman and an artist in the twentieth century." One senses that not only does Spark's creation mean it, so too must have Spark, who fashioned a sly prayer for the writer in her poem "To the Gods of My Right Hand": "Whoever the gods, / let them enter my right hand, never / to forget her cunning in the first and the last encounter."

Cunning: Spark cunningly attended to the dramatic potential of failure in her fiction. Without potential failure, there can be no creative tension. To defend against her own failure as a writer also required cunning, as well as a disciplined work ethic. At the age of eighty-five Spark confessed that she still felt guilty if she didn't write daily.

Just the Right Amount of Failure, Please

"AMBITION IS THE LAST REFUGE OF FAILURE."— OSCAR WILDE

There are so many ways to flub even the most rudimentary literary effect. Plodding narration or cleverness that gets tiring. Or the draft is underdeveloped. Or the novel is over-stuffed. Then too, there are always dilemmas about characters. Even guilt over killing characters can be a stumbling block. Think of J. K. Rowling and the pressure she endured before she ended the Harry Potter series. Begged not to kill fictional children.

It's not easy to entertain Joyce Carol Oates's musings about failure. In *The Faith of the Writer*, in which her essay "Notes on Failure" appears, we can be forgiven for counting the number of volumes listed as "Also by Joyce Carol Oates." What could such a prolific writer offer on the topic of failure? The words of T. S. Eliot, for one example, as she informs us that, "When it was observed to T. S. Eliot that most critics are failed writers, Eliot replied: 'But so are most writers.'" In turn, Oates provides us with a sense of how ambition can make the possibility of failure both a prod to increased production and a perverse but faithful source of intimacy: "Success is distant and illusory, failure one's loyal companion, one's stimulus for imagining that the next book will be better for, otherwise, why write?"

A young writer I know claims that *Pinocchio* is any author's true story. She's right, but the writer isn't only Pinocchio, that adventurer who longs to explore possibilities previously unknown. Nor are writers only or entirely like the wild boys in Pinocchio's story, although no writer can ever fully determine what mischief characters might be up to in the minds of readers. No, the writer is also Geppetto, who wants to make a real boy. The writer, like Geppetto, is swallowed by the whale of the book, not the reverse. The book gets big and the writer feels transparent and afloat, overwhelmed and newly strange. It feels like a triumph sometimes just to stay alive in the thing.

To stay alive in the thing is both the writer's and the reader's challenge.

Erasing All Over Again

I remember riding in a car with two other women who were talking about a writer. "I admire her. She's written books."

Silence in the car.

The woman continued, "The weird thing is, so have I. It just doesn't feel like I have."

I don't think that this was a case of modesty or self-denigration. Every new book, as the adage goes, means starting over again. Actually, writing can be more like erasing all over again. As if what is written is written to be freed. There is a peculiar cleansing quality about writing. To make is to unmake, to untie a very tight knot. The urge to write may have to do with a powerful form of forgetting, of loosening certain perspectives, of banishing some of the more restricting bands of identity. That too can be a form of ambition. Zadie Smith makes a point that bears on this:

> "*My god, I was a different person!*"—yes, all writers think this from book to book … After each book is done, I look forward to hating it (and never have to wait long); I get a weird, inverse confidence from feeling destroyed, because being destroyed, having to start again, means I have space in front of me, somewhere to go.

The self that Yeats talked about remaking in every line gets remade so utterly that with each book "a different person" emerges, or at least the flickering perception of a rebirth. Or another less sanguine possibility exists. What occurs is rejection of the previous self, flawed and searching, the self cast off in favor of the next writing self, a new and more sterling phantom.

Christian Wiman, in *Ambition and Survival*, notes how the most ambitious writing life can peel away hard-held suppositions about even our most fundamental beliefs:

> [T]he ambition and fierce focus, the hunger of it, the sense of a life shaped by some strong inner imperative: all of this— even the moments easy to mock, even the years when I wrote only bad poems, or no poems—I find myself cherishing. I still believe that a life in poetry demands absolutely everything—including, it has turned out for me, the belief that a life in poetry demands absolutely everything.

Further into the realm of erasing assumptions, we can think of the writer as a phantom whenever engaged in the act of writing. Drawing on Henry James's story "The Private Life," in which the public persona of any writer is described as a ghost-self, Cynthia Ozick argues the reverse: "It's not the social personality who is the ghost; it is the writer with shoulders bent over paper, the hazy simulacrum whom we will never personally know, the wraith who hides out in the dark while her palpable effigy walks abroad, talking and circulating and sometimes even flirting." We are our social opposites when we write, Ozick argues. The braggart in public is "a helpless milquetoast" before the page or screen. "And that apologetically obsequious, self-effacing, breathlessly diffident and deprecatory creature turns out, when in the trancelike grip of nocturnal ardor, to be a fiery furnace of unopposable authority and galloping certainty." In Ozick's formulation, we write "against type." A writing life is at the very least a double life. It is a life in which not only memory but also forgetfulness has value.

Rescue This Man

Whether I've written on buses, at dining room tables, on fold-out couches, at desks of varying vintages, on a balcony perched over a busy street, I tend to remember where I was writing more clearly than how I managed to engender a plot. I remember the decor in the coffee shop in Stone Harbor, New Jersey, where I wrote parts of *The Guide to the Flying Island* better than I remember how I devised the novella's progression of scenes.

I've called this book *Swallowing the Sea*. But when I'm writing it's more like the sea swallows me. And afterward, no matter how much a book took over my life, I often forget how I arrived at certain solutions to the book's inevitable challenges.

Comfortingly, the Nobel Laureate Juan Ramón Jiménez says, "In the poetic imagination, as in the sea, there may be zones of forgetting, but nothing is ever lost." He also says—profoundly, I believe—"Forgetting loses nothing; it stores everything up like treasure. And if we are worthy of memory, she will give us the key to forgetting."

Inevitably my memory, particularly my sense memory, guides aspects of my writing. To range beyond memory and to imagine most deeply, particularly in short stories or longer fiction, I use distancing devices to dissolve the contours of my own life. I give myself ways to forget myself so that the unknown has room to crack through the surface of what I know.

In *The Guide to the Flying Island,* the central character witnesses a woman fall, or leap, or somehow mysteriously disappear from an island's cliff. He searches for the woman, changing his life as he searches, even while everyone he knows doubts that the woman ever existed. Writing that novella was one of the happiest experiences of my writing life, and the ending surprised and fulfilled me in ways I can hardly explain. What allowed me to surprise myself in the course of writing, I believe now, was a certain forgetfulness achieved through simple means.

The main character in *The Guide to the Flying Island* is a shy, tall, large-bodied man who operates a tour boat. I happen to be a not particularly shy woman of average height who has never operated a boat or led a tour. As a consequence, my censors—ever-vigilant and demanding—were partly disabled. I wasn't writing even remotely about someone like myself, so how could my censors feel embarrassed and defensive on my behalf?

While I freed myself to live in the mind of a character whose outer circumstances bore no resemblance to my own, other elements of the novella were not derived from distancing devices that fostered self-forgetfulness but from emotional memory. I wrote from a sympathy for and an intimate knowledge of some of my character's obsessions. I honored his sensitivity to abandonment, his reluctance to be drawn into the past, his awe before beauty. But because those emotions were lodged in a big-bodied man, I felt especially free to imagine my way into his world, to engage in the sort of all-out self-forgetfulness that is one of the satisfactions writing offers.

After the book was finished, after I had lingered in my character's consuming passions, including those passions not identical to my own, I knew that if I was ever going to write anything else I had to try to forget that man. I left him on his island.

His name is Jake Isinglass.

Slow Insults: Is Your Writing Trying to Insult You?

When I consider words that may be most vividly remembered, insults assume special prominence.

An insult is a brain spike that seeks to embed itself and put a new narrative into circulation. An insult is a device fitted with an explosive charge for wounding identity. Like art, insults want to be remembered.

A common phenomenon interests me here. I call it The Slow Insult. That is, there are insults that take hours, days, months, even years to register. The insult itself may have been inventive and brilliant or crude and juvenile, but the target doesn't initially register the insult. I can offer a very simple example of an insult that took decades for me to register. I was a first-year college student when a man asked to draw my picture in the student cafeteria. I sat for him while he sketched. Afterward he complimented me. Gratified, I told another student about the man's compliment. She said three simple words: "Is he sick?"

Only recently did that incident from college come floating into my consciousness again, for no reason I know. Even after so many years, recalling what that young woman said and at last understanding her irony, I felt a twinge. How many other insults had I missed? I remember, too, the look on the young woman's face when her insult didn't register: Pained. At the time, I thought she was worried about that guy's health.

Writing is a good place for far better-made insults. Insults are where power may lie—particularly the insult launched as a threat to the victim's integrity. Inexperienced writers who pamper their characters protect them from insults. Actual life protects no one. Apparently no one of any age. I was watching when a baby less than a month old, held in the arms of her mother, was told, "Hey, sweetie, why did Mommy and Daddy give you that funky name?"

Making a resounding insult in art—rather than insults directed toward babies and their parents—can be seductive, evidenced by writers who have been attracted to the practice. As if to establish proof, there's a vigorous industry in cataloguing Shakespeare's insults, with multiple sites on the Internet, for example *www.william-shakespeare.org*, which has alphabetized listings of his more chewy insults from *A* (including "Annointed Sovereign of Sighs and Groans," "Arrant counterfeit rascal," "Ass-head") to *Y* (including "Your peevish chastity is not worth a breakfast in the cheapest country").

Art can work by delivering its insults to the brain in delayed fashion, which may be a reason to re-read. We have endured the impression that we've missed something, that there is for us—in bondage to curiosity—more for us to discover. What I'm focusing on by mentioning slow insults is the mind's ability to bundle and suppress meaning, then progressively deliver insight. In other words, I'm claiming for writers the ambition of making insults to the brain, although those insults may sometimes be delivered slowly. Then, too, there's another way in which slow insults work: A character may not know he or she has been insulted, but the reader knows and delights in the knowledge.

The Land of Undone? I Designed the Flag

Sometimes people joke about the title of one of my books, *Undid in the Land of Undone*. "The Land of Undone? That's my homeland," they say. "The Land of Undone? I'm its leading citizen." The title poem reflects my preoccupation with regret and with earnest effort misapplied:

> All the things I wanted to do and didn't
> took so long.
> It was years of not doing.
>
> You can make an allusion here to Penelope,
> if you want.
> See her up there in that high room undoing her art?
>
> But enough about what she didn't do—
> not doing
> was what she did. Plucking out
>
> the thread of intimacy in the frame.
> So let's make a toast to the long art
> of lingering. We say the cake is done,
>
> but what exactly did the cake do?
> The things undid
> in the land of undone call to us
>
> in the flames. What I didn't do took
> an eternity—
> and it wasn't for lack of trying.

Since appearing in a literary magazine, the poem has lived a migratory existence. Its lines ("let's make a toast to the long art / of lingering") popped up, properly credited, in a calendar square inside Oprah Winfrey's magazine *O*, and in a country inn's website announcement of a wine-tasting. While the poem is accumulating a past on the Internet, the past that's figured within the poem never extinguishes the flames on the Land of Undone, where I can no longer rescue all I didn't do or did not choose to do.

I like to tell myself that what's undone doesn't only live in the past. On the farther shore of the Land of Undone looms the future. Everything any of us might imagine waits there, for better or, even, for worse.

BOREDOM

Gray Jelly

I am being kept from something.

Consciousness submerges itself in gray jelly.

I'm not sleepy. No, boredom requires an itchy sort of alertness.

I am here and I am bored.

To bring up boredom is terribly delicate. You feel so boring. And you stand accused, as I do now. As others have before me. Years ago a nice man was complaining to me about how boring a professor we both had was—how boring, so boring, how really deeply truly boring the professor was—and I said to that nice man in front of me who was complaining of being bored—I said, without meaning to, it just popped out, horrifyingly enough, in the manner of a swift, unmistakable, unintentional insult—I said: "You're boring."

Boredom. We wish to escape, but we are blocked by good manners, and those hostile sentinels: Social obligation. Human charity. Oppressive arrangements.

Boredom is like obscenity. Different standards apply. What bores one does not bore another. As with pornography, what stimulates you may not stimulate a judge. Even celebrity gossip can be boring and predictable, which is why the deflationary line that closes Frank O'Hara's poem about a celebrity's fainting spell never dims: "oh Lana Turner we love you get up."

Boredom, in its most abominable aspect, can be a condition generated by immovable structures that do not respond to human needs other than through suppression. Martin Amis notes, "Terror and boredom are very old friends, as onetime residents of Russia (and other countries) will uneasily recall." In *Humboldt's Gift*, Saul Bellow's character Charlie Citrine, who regularly contemplates writing an essay on boredom, makes a similar argument: "What—in other words—would modern boredom be without terror? One of the most boring documents of all time is the thick volume of *Hitler's Table Talk.*" Likewise, in his novel *Boredom*, Alberto Moravia's protagonist remarks of oppression, "Boredom, which is the lack of a relationship with external things, was in the very air one breathed during the period of Fascism." For Moravia's character, boredom is contended with viscerally:

> Reality, when I am bored, has always had the same disconcerting effect upon me as (to use a metaphor) a too-short blanket has upon a sleeping man on a winter night: he pulls it down over his feet and his chest gets cold, then he pulls it up on to his chest and his feet get cold, and so he never succeeds in falling properly asleep.

In another inspired comparison, Moravia describes boredom as "a withering process; an almost instantaneous loss of vitality—just as though one saw a flower change in a few seconds from a bud to decay and dust."

Moravia's analogy has recently gained credibility from scientists. According to researchers at the Department of Epidemiology and Public Health at University College London, boredom may literally wither us. Jonathan Petre in the *Daily Mail* reported that "[m]ore than 7,000 civil servants were studied over 25 years—and those who said they were bored were nearly 40 percent more likely to have died by the end of the study than those who did not." One of the primary researchers, Martin Shipley, counseled people to "find outside interests."

Don't be idle.

"Idle hands make mischief."

So do busy hands.

So do (or should) a writer's hands. If only to defend against—
or to represent faithfully—boredom.

Jane Austen Completely Covered in Quills

The English novelist Ivy Compton-Burnett (1884–1969) special-
ized in boredom within upper-middle-class families. Her novels
dissect the Edwardian family in which the unquestioned rights of
fathers and the laws of inheritance effectively installed dictatorial
regimes with restless subjects: wives, children, and poor relatives. In-
cest in her fiction literalizes patterns that are already at work in her
despots' desires to replicate themselves. Out of her characters' failed
attempts to defend themselves against the relentless predictability of
domestic tyrants, Compton-Burnett made her prickly fiction.

Certain names crop up when critics compare her to other writers,
among them Lewis Carroll, Oscar Wilde, and Jane Austen. But it's
Lewis Carroll as if the Red Queen executed his plots. And it's Oscar
Wilde without his exuberant delight. And it's Jane Austen if she were
completely covered in quills.

I'm not aware of any other fiction writer who uses dialogue so
exclusively and at the same time so obsessively interrogates her char-
acters' words. Her novels are composed almost entirely of dialogue,
with few speech tags to orient us. She unbraids and rebraids clichés.
"People who remember things, always remember them as if they were
yesterday," claims one of her characters, adding, "I remember it as if
it were twenty-six years ago." One character says to another: "I would
not have you rise to the occasion. I should feel you were someone else."

Her novels are a little like *Lord of the Flies,* if almost everyone seated around the dinner table is poor murdered Piggy. While family tyrants enforce their suffocating, claustrophobic regimes on their victims, the tyrants' language is characterized by its infantilism, its grasping, its capacity to bore other characters when not horrifying them. Of course the Edwardian machinations of power that Compton-Burnett witheringly conveys aren't foreign to our age. Autocrats continue across time, ruling by suspicion and demanding flattery and sympathy. Those oppressive techniques work not only within a family but on a far larger stage. Terror, once again in Martin Amis's terms, wields its power alongside boredom.

Admittedly, certain novelistic satisfactions aren't available to Compton-Burnett's readers, including immersion in a sense of place or a dynamic view of time passing. A Compton-Burnett character's nature may be revealed but seldom changed. We hardly learn any information about the factual world, although we may be introduced obliquely to obsolete inheritance laws.

The intense concentration that reading such fiction requires creates its own uncanny reward, for Compton-Burnett had the timing of an exceptionally morbid stand-up comic fascinated by abuses of power. The filmmaker John Waters thoroughly appreciates the distinctive experience of reading her, as he explains in *Role Models*:

> Right up to the end of her life, Ivy Compton-Burnett's irritable, nitpicking, obsessive love of words never ceased. According to the great biography *Ivy*, by Hilary Spurling, an old friend came to visit Ivy and she woke up from a catnap and snapped, "I'm not tired, I'm sleepy. They are different things. And I'm surprised that you should say tired when you mean sleepy."... Her last spoken words before death? "Leave me alone." I have to. I have all twenty of her novels and I've read nineteen. If I read the one that is left there will be no more Ivy Compton-Burnett for me and I will probably have to die myself.

Writing: Revenge on Boredom

Boredom has a way of coming for writers—as incitement, as plot catalyst, as technical challenge, or as an interviewer. Think of actual writers, annoyed with interviewers, bored with interviewers' questions, high-handed and imperious writers. Gore Vidal?

Many of us write to escape boredom. We certainly don't write to guarantee it. The irony is that writing requires both ambition and a tolerance for inertia, for enduring boredom when a manuscript stalls, and for cultivating an understanding of boredom as it must be represented or defended against. A writer must rinse out the trough of expectation and turn boring moments into functional ones.

Henry James in "The Art of Fiction" explores the obligation to beat back boredom as the artist's central responsibility: "But the only condition that I can think of attaching to the composition of the novel is, as I have already said, that it be interesting. This freedom is a splendid privilege, and the first lesson of the young novelist is to learn to be worthy of it." That is a great deal to ask.

Jane Austen ought to rear up her head about now as the writer best able to render incidents of boredom riveting in the telling. She marches her bores around until they're good-time bores. Her novels are guidebooks to squeezing out the illicit pleasures that boring people offer. If each of her heroines could move beyond boring obstacles (some of her relatives or the toadies in her life), fresh opportunities would meet her at least halfway. Unfortunately for her, although temporarily, our heroine is stuck in a taffy vat.

Northanger Abbey, Austen's first novel but her last to be published, scrutinizes the boredom of self-inflation and of triviality, to heroine Catherine Morland's dismay and for the reader's pleasure. Think of Mrs. Allen who "congratulated herself, as soon as ... seated, on having preserved her gown from injury," a woman who judges every circumstance in terms of the participants' attire. And worse yet, in the same novel exists John Thorpe—horse-obsessed, buffoonish, an exaggerator of the first rank who exemplifies the boredom that liars generate. As anyone who has encountered a practiced and unrepentant liar knows, a terrible boredom attaches to listening to one. A compulsive liar's lies are the dullest of lies. A realist might say that that's why so many political speeches are boring.

For many, I suspect, boredom is a stalled form of ambition: ambition to be elsewhere, and to be otherwise. To stop reality from impinging in a particular way. It's not about having nothing to do—there are always things that can be done—it's about not being responsive to the things that could be done. Adam Phillips in *On Kissing, Tickling, and Being Bored: Psychoanalytic Essays on the Unexamined Life* calls boredom "that state of suspended animation in which things are started and nothing begins, the mood of diffuse restlessness which contains that most absurd and paradoxical wish, the wish for a desire."

Boredom: a depletion that gets filled with irritation, and penetrated by needles of self-castigation.

Frankly, I have almost no tolerance for boredom. It's an inherited incapacity. My mother couldn't bear boredom either. During one awkward lull in the conversation with stiff, prim acquaintances she tried to stir things up by saying, "I once saw a man completely covered in warts." When she was bored she often used the phrase "A little of this goes a long way." I can't begin to count how many times I've silently repeated those words to myself.

ξ

In *The Atlantic*'s New Ideas Issue of 2010 the novelist Walter Kirn argues that "boredom is extinct." The means of extinction are "Twitter, iPads, Blackberrys, voice-activation in-dash navigation systems and a hundred other technologies that offer distraction anywhere, anytime." As a result, Kirn states, boredom has become in large part "a memory." Why isn't Kirn's argument persuasive? Maybe because everything is not illuminated, not even by an illuminated screen. Our direct experience shows many of us that we have a capacity for boredom that can defeat the most ingenious diversions.

Seemingly, we shouldn't take for granted how stubbornly tedious boredom can be. Kirn argues that boredom once led to daydreams (which are now, he argues, becoming as extinct as boredom). But even that formulation is problematic. Boredom doesn't necessarily lead to daydreaming any more than insomnia leads to inspiration. For many of us, boredom and insomnia both occupy dead zones. And even if Kirn were to be correct about the boredom-busting potential of electronic devices, it can't be true that every situation allows us to access those devices and thus to keep boredom at bay. It's hard to sneak texting into committee meetings. Or classroom lectures—if you're giving one. Or if you're waiting on tables or working in the Department of Motor Vehicles. Boredom is an invasive species, and both our temporary defeat of boredom and our capitulation to boredom are recorded in the fossil records of our books—and on our blogs, too: endlessly.

ξ

The last novel David Foster Wallace worked on, *The Pale King*, is a study of boredom among Internal Revenue Service agents. According to the *New Yorker*, the novel caused Wallace immense trouble for its "many ambitions," given that the novel "would show people a way to insulate themselves from the toxic freneticism of American life. It had to be emotionally engaged and morally sound, and to narrate boredom while obeying the physics of reading." In "Wiggle Room," a portion of the manuscript first published in the *New Yorker*, Wallace describes boredom through his IRS-agent character: "He had the sensation of a great type of hole or emptiness falling through him and continuing to fall and never hitting the floor." The sensation of falling that Wallace describes strikes me as especially apt, for boredom is experienced as if it defies the laws of nature. Time doesn't pass so much as assume weight. Wallace's description sounds somewhat like the converse of *Alice's Adventures in Wonderland*. Alice falls through a hole and keeps falling for a very long time. The hole doesn't fall through her. Essentially, though, both Lewis Carroll's and Wallace's plots are about boredom. Carroll's is a book, after all, about a child who is bored because her sister is sitting on a riverbank reading a book. *Alice's Adventures in Wonderland* can be both exhilarating and myopically focused on the helplessness we feel in situations that defy every known remedy, frustrating us to the point of despondency and torpor.

Boredom, as Harold Schweizer argues in *On Waiting*, is not the same as waiting, for "waiting differs ... from the mental relaxation in boredom" (although some people experience boredom, as I do, as anything but relaxing, as a kind of gripping sludge). Of course boredom has its different effects on behavior and those effects may involve waiting for reality to shift. When bored, I find myself walking around innocent objects and hating them, begging them: *Why don't you suggest something?* We may experience our boredom as if it deflates the world. On a boring summer day even petunias seem like those melted timepieces in Salvador Dali paintings. Boredom is, I've heard, a luxury. No. Frankly, it's not.

We all have our varieties of boring experiences. What follows are the closest I can come to delivering examples of nearly universal boredom in the Western world, examples that are particularly resistant to explanation:

1) Insanely embroidered narratives about people we don't know and never will whose lives are inherently undramatic but divinely ordained to suggest our own inadequacies.

2) Committees. Even the spelling of the word warns of duplicated efforts: two *m*'s, two *t*'s, two *e*'s. *Committee:* mediocrity takes up the shovel. Someone brings doughnuts—as if that ever solved anything. (Medusa attracts more poets than the hydra, even though the hydra has more heads. Why? The medusa was a beautiful woman whose luck ran bad. The hydra was a committee.)

3) Dreams. Boring to anyone but the dreamer. The six most dreaded words in the English language: "Let me tell you my dream."

4) Commencement speeches. Even the best begin with an apology and a promise, false, of brevity. Which is why, possibly, Joseph Brodsky decided to confront the matter head on and concoct one of the few surprising efforts ever made in the genre when in 1989 he gave the commencement speech at Dartmouth. He sprinkled the proud graduates with the following: "The only way art can become for you a solace from boredom, from the existential equivalent of a cliché, is if you yourselves become artists. Given your number, though, this prospect is as unappetizing as it is unlikely." Boredom, he went on, offers the ultimate tutelage: "the lesson of your utter insignificance." He concluded: "I doubt you'll ever have it better than here."

5) Any communication that believes in its own clichés:

> Writing that magnetizes a cliché.
> Writing that reupholsters a cliché.
> Writing that doesn't know it's a cliché.
> Writing that knows it's a cliché, but figures that, as such, it contains a grain of immortality.

Boredom, Boredom Everywhere, and Every Drop I Drink

When boredom is given serious analytical treatment (as opposed to treatment that resorts to anecdote, allegory, analogy, and complaints—I stand accused) more often than not a puzzling thing happens. Boredom becomes a miasma that overtakes all narrated experience, an infecting blob of humorlessness. As Patricia Meyer Spacks claims in *Boredom: The Literary History of a State of Mind,* imaginative writing must continually contend with boredom as part of the contemporary condition. She argues that "The expanding definition of boredom in our own time means that by now one might argue that virtually every work currently written speaks of the condition in one way or another." Boredom, it seems, is the ultimate imperialist, subsuming all in its flabby wave. She further maintains that "As action and as product, writing resists boredom, constituting itself by that resistance. In this sense all writing—at least since 1800 or so—is about boredom." In *Experience Without Qualities: Boredom and Modernity,* Elizabeth S. Goodstein goes further, describing boredom as an ultimate implosion of meaning: "Self and world collapse in a nihilistic affirmation that nothing means, nothing pleases, nothing matters."

More recently, Peter Toohey's *Boredom: A Lively History* amounts to a recuperation of boredom, although he spends a good deal of time with remedies for conquering boredom which, as Joseph Epstein cleverly points out in a *Commentary* review of Toohey's book, tend to sound boring in such a context: sociability, music, aerobic exercise. Toohey finds boredom to be an internal warning system, ringing the bell on our need to alter our ways: "Boredom may drive thinkers and artists to question the accepted and to search for change." At the same time, he can't resist cutting other thinkers' and artists' conceptions of boredom down to size, arguing against the propensity "to render [boredom] alarmingly significant by endowing it with philosophical accoutrements." Certainly he can't be accused of inflating boredom in light of his book's deflationary final sentence: "Boredom simply deserves respect for the, well, boring experience that it is."

The most perversely entertaining study of boredom of which I'm aware is Lars Svendsen's *A Philosophy of Boredom*, first published in English in 2005. Even Svendsen's narrative about how he began to write about boredom is charming—although I can't tell if the charm comes from my failure to read the book in the original language, or if I'm reading a study that is tongue-in-cheek at virtually all moments. Consider the fluid sense of self-aggrandizement in this line: "My intention is in no way to reduce all of life to being an expression of boredom." And who can help but try to imagine the plight of the author's friends to whom he was "virtually unable to talk about anything else other than the subject of this book"? With a summary assertion, Svendsen makes clear his allegiance to the common academic argument that boredom is all-encompassing: "Boredom has to be accepted as an unavoidable fact, as life's own gravity. This is no grand solution, for the problem of boredom has none." Earlier in the book he had cultivated greater uncertainty: "I carried out a small, unscientific survey among colleagues, students, friends and acquaintances that revealed that they were on the whole unable to say whether they were bored or not." Aptly, Svendsen quotes Lord Byron: "There's little left but to be bored or bore." I, too, conducted a spontaneous survey focused on one person—an eighteen-year-old. "How often are you bored," I asked her. "I'm never bored," she said.

Now what do I do?

What if Svendsen and Byron are right about the ubiquity of boredom? They have plenty of other writers on their side, including those using boredom as a plot device and a theme to maneuver the imagination. Boredom is not only a catalyst of adultery in novels— the supposed cure for actual boredom in centuries allegedly more stupid than our own—but boredom is so widespread a concern for writers that it not only seeps across the centuries but into the non-human realm. Theodore Roethke begins "Dolor" with an anthem to "the inexorable sadness of pencils." Rainer Maria Rilke's "The Panther," translated here by David Young, is the most penetrating poem to caged energy ever composed:

> Once in a while the curtain of the pupil
> parts silently——. An image goes in then,
> runs through the trembling stillness of the limbs
> and vanishes inside the heart.

In Philip Larkin's "Dockery and Son," boredom gets supplanted:

> Life is first boredom, then fear.
> Whether or not we use it, it goes,
> And leaves what something hidden from us chose,
> And age, and then the only end of age.

It could be that boredom is represented in literature as one of the least expensive status symbols, given that boredom is sometimes attached to suggestions of superior intelligence. The easily bored are thought to comprehend all too well our routine satisfactions and are un-stimulated by life's common demands.

Something otherworldly attaches itself to boredom, which is why the bored are sometimes called "world-weary," like the gifted actor George Sanders, best known as the jaded theater critic in *All About Eve* and as Rebecca's sinful, hood-eyed "cousin" in Hitchcock's *Rebecca.*

Sanders brought into being characters of menacing sophistication who give off an infernal impression of being perpetually and petulantly omniscient. "Dear World, I am leaving because I am bored" is the first line of the short suicide note written by Sanders himself. Tragic as it is, Sanders's note is perfectly in keeping with his indelible creations, his perpetually bored characters who cannot bore us.

There is, of course, the other equation about boredom, like the one the mother makes in John Berryman's most famous "Dream Song." As you may recall, the poem begins, "Life, friends, is boring." Following up, his boring mother tells him "Ever to confess you're bored / means you have no // Inner Resources." That precept remains popular: To be easily bored is the sign of superficiality. Writers of imaginative literature, of course, must beat back those charges, particularly the charge of frivolousness, the charge of creating only diversions to defeat momentarily the boredom of those who lack the ability to do something useful that impinges on reality.

Although as W. H. Auden wrote, "never / to be dull shows a lack of taste," no one wants to be boring. And defeating boredom is not simply a matter of developing an allergy to repetition. The familiar is calming, reassuring, repeatedly gratifying. We don't read Anita Brooker for a new plot, after all; we return for another perspective on a similar situation in which a rather familiar woman finds herself absorbed, and in which the author is absorbed.

Yet for me, at least, it is almost impossible to continue to write imaginative work if I'm bored by the scene or the situation or the characters. Boredom of that sort doesn't necessarily derive from familiarity as much as from a feeling that all options are blocked. The common cure you'll find in writing guides for this malady tends to be: Add a character. This works in life too, though possibly with disastrous results.

To avoid boredom in our writing, some of us continually devise more challenges for our characters—another typical suggestion of how-to books. Maybe we're like Clara in Steven Millhauser's short story "Dangerous Laughter" in which teenagers are so bored they hold what they call "laughing parties." Clara, a genius of laughter, will not let her talent go to waste even after the parties lose their luster and "a passion for weeping" overcomes the other young people. Clara stays in the laughing game, not the weeping game, becoming ever more ambitious and finally outdoing herself and all comers. She laughs herself to death. The wages of ambition? Or of boredom?

Sometimes I've made the worst possible choices when fearing boredom as I write. I compose wilder scenes, quickening the pace with incidents. I fantasize about inserting into the plot car chases that occur in unpredictable locations—say, on a highway made slippery by an overturned semi hauling bacon. I am tempted to make characters even weirder, although too weird is, oddly, boring.

One of the best pieces of advice about writing that I've ever received, although I resented it at the time given that it was directed at me personally, was composed of one word: *Relax.*

Instead of creating more complications, it's more likely that I need to slow down, to inhabit a scene more deeply, to re-live what words intimate, even to begin again at the start of the work and listen harder until I hear breathing in the labyrinth.

But what if boredom with the work still persists? Boredom might be a legitimate indicator that the writer should abandon a project. Or more likely boredom means that the deeper implications are as yet unrealized in the work and, in my case, I may have numbed myself to those implications. As such, boredom should be suspect. It can be the mask under which the secret of the work is hidden.

How to strip away that subterfuge? It might be especially useful to identify and focus on an obsession.

Writers tend to trade in obsessions. How else would a book ever get written? But an obsession within a piece of writing may not be immediately visible, particularly to the writer. To discover an obsession calls for what I call extreme listening. Reading by listening. Reading the writing aloud. Asking:

> *What is the writing trying to tell me?*
> *What is buzzing around among and between the words?*
> *How can I rediscover my characters' obsessions by taking stock*
> *of my own?*

An obsession remains an obsession because of intuitions that lead us to attempt to find language for what is already escaping us, for mysteries that retain their mysteriousness, for inchoate cravings that aren't fulfilled.

There have been times when I've thought of writing as a pocket of breath in an avalanche. In the cold onrush of a life's demands, the time and space for writing may seem as rare as that pocket of breath. To do justice to what we intuit may seem impossible; so much resists language. A series of sentences floating in the white space of *Writing*, the screenwriter and novelist Marguerite Duras's prose meditations, follows a progression that faces these quandaries and quietly overcomes them:

> To write.
> I can't.
> No one can.
> We have to admit: we cannot.
> And yet we write.

A Road Trip with Ahab

Obsession and the creative exploration of obsession can be the answer—for some—for defeating the writer's boredom and the reader's. In lived experience, however, obsession may be paralyzing. During a long car ride, an actual Ahab might bore you to death. Or Gatsby: his naiveté is fascinating, but for how long? Another sad party, yet again? Wouldn't Nick Carraway at some point have dumped Gatsby no matter what happened? It's the quality of desire, combined with the inherent complexity of the person doing the desiring, that can make a character rise above boredom.

The question "What bores your character?" can be a useful one—especially if we consider how often tragedy and comedy evolve from the desire to avoid boredom. Boredom is, after all, a plot device, and characters may develop obsessions to overcome their sense of claustrophobia or inertia. We have only to think of Madame Bovary and her tragic, velvety boredom. Or Anna Karenina's quivering, sultry boredom. Or Effi Briest's fretting, juvenile boredom. Boredom is a register of personality and a subterranean motivation for many characters. Is Iago bored? Is Othello his Malvolio, and in another incarnation could Iago be Toby Belch? How dismal to live with an actual human Malvolio, but how delicious to lambaste him in writing—up to a certain point, until we find our sympathies pricked.

"I'll Bite You Myself"

Which brings me to *The Wizard of Oz*, that epic of opposition to boredom and sensible resignation, as so many children's books and films are, or profess to be, or become in the imagination of the adults who read or view them. Perhaps plenty of writers find the film *The Wizard of Oz* endearing because it contains lines that constitute testimonials about writing:

> "There goes some of me again."
> "I haven't any courage at all. I even scare myself."
> "That's you all over."
> "Oh joy, rapture, I've got a brain."
> "I'll bite you myself."

I identified with the *The Wizard of Oz*—a farm child's story—in part because of my own circumstances. I spent my childhood on a mid-Michigan farm in the midst of beauty and strangeness. My sister Lana and I caught bullheads in the creek at the bottom of the hill below our farm, running back up the hill with the fish in a bucket and pouring them into a horse tank where we watched them wave their sleek black horns under the water. Behind the barn flowed a stream where tall reeds hissed in the wind. Farther back spread a meadow where I ran in the clover pretending to be a nymph after I became enchanted with Herman J. Wechsler's *Gods and Goddesses in Art and Legend* and its grainy images of naked, soft-bellied goddesses. Throughout the woods in spring were expanses of yellow trout lilies, jack-in-the-pulpits, lady slippers, and trillium with startlingly white petals broad as handkerchiefs.

One very early morning my mother took my hand and led me to a lot where a cow was penned. A tiny set of legs jutted out from under the cow's tail. "That's the way you came out," my mother said. "Backwards. A breech birth. Just like that. I want you to remember this." As if I could forget.

There were so many births. Piglets swarming, nosing through straw. More calves, their eyes bulbous and almost purple. Separated from their mothers, the calves pulled so hard at the pails of milk I brought them that they nearly toppled me.

There was death, too. A gang of turkey vultures used our silo as a rest stop, their heads drooping, as if exhausted from their long gliding forays. In the woods I discovered a dead heifer, her legs sticking straight up, her body bloated to the size of a piano. One afternoon in early summer, Lana and I were perched on a grassy hillock that overlooked Wacousta Road when a truck passed below us filled with dead farm animals, mostly steers and sheep. Squeezed in between the other bodies were pigs, like pink filler.

We also knew boredom, boredom that is palpable in Dorothy's farm world in *The Wizard of Oz*. For us, boredom arrived in late summer. Some afternoons I was so bored I used to sit in the fork of a tree counting passing cars. It's hard to convey our excitement when we knew that *The Wizard of Oz* was coming on television—when a tornado was made magnificent and never seriously harmed anyone except for a house-crushed witch, when a child (although it is always hard to think of Judy Garland as a child; she's more like some evanescent higher being) overcomes both human and magical detractors; and when that child steps into a landscape of lozenges and lily pads in her matte-black, sensible shoes, relics from a blown-away realm of pinched irritability, from boring, wistful afternoons.

Writers have claimed the story in idiosyncratic ways. Ray Bradbury bizarrely reflected that the author of the Oz books, L. Frank Baum, is "that faintly old-maidish man who grew boys inward to their most delightful interiors, kept them home, and romanced them with wonder between their ears" where "Love is the lubricant." For John Updike, "Baum invented escapism without escape," as well as "a refreshingly agnostic fantasy." To my mind, the most resonant appreciation of the film is Salman Rushdie's, written while he was under the *fatwa*, surviving in an atmosphere that must have been rife with the constraints of what Martin Amis in another context calls "boredom and terror." The agonies of enduring his repressive situation inform Rushdie's meditation on the film, which he counts as his "very first literary influence," its "driving force the inadequacy of adults."

Often the wizard is seen as a prototype of the writer who is good with special effects and uncanny illusions. But it's not the wizard who interests me, the illusionist or artist/manipulator sent away in a puff of air. Nor is it the witch who intrigues me most, despite her spectacular troop of flying monkeys. For me, it is Dorothy who offers the more appealing image of a writer—the one who takes her boredom and rolls it into a ball and blasts herself out of a drab world. In Rushdie's reading, the boredom of Kansas is obliterated in early scenes by the force of Dorothy's will: "The tornado is the grayness gathered together and whirled about and unleashed, so to speak, against itself." Rushdie argues that "in many ways Dorothy is the gale blowing through this little corner of nowhere, demanding justice for her little dog while the adults give in meekly to the powerful Miss Gulch." Wind-tossed Dorothy's experience resembles a writer's own, as Marguerite Duras defines it:

> Writing comes like the wind. It's naked, it's made of ink, it's the thing written, and it passes like nothing else passes in life, nothing more, except life itself.

At the film's conclusion, when Dorothy finds herself back in Kansas and expounds on the virtues of home, Rushdie revolts. He objects to the film's "cloying ending," which he argues is "untrue to the film's anarchic spirit." He's right about the return of repression, although Aunt Em, that embodiment of worry and resignation, can't help but dismiss Dorothy's vision, given the constraints of her own harried and impoverished life. "Lie quiet now. You just had a bad dream," she tells Dorothy, who has undergone something on the order of an alien abduction.

Note this progression of a few key lines at the very end of the film:

"I did leave you."

"You just had a bad dream."

"We dream lots of silly things."

"But most of it was beautiful."

"You're all here. I'm not going to leave here ever ever again. Because I love you all. Oh, Auntie Em, there's no place like home."

Garland gives the film's ending the ring of astonishment. A dingy evil has been defeated almost by accident—and guiltlessly, as Rushdie and others note. There's no place like home, but there's no place like Oz either. Early in the movie Miss Gulch tells us: "Now you see reason." Yes, this is what reason looks like: hatchet-faced, skeletal, unforgiving. Dorothy, on the other hand, discovers how to be heroic and handle a broomstick without having to sweep the floor with it.

A lie can make us recognize just how well Dorothy serves as a prototype for writers. Plenty of lies buzz around in the film. The most telling comes from the Good Witch Glinda who, near the end, tells Dorothy: "You've always had the power to go back to Kansas." Functioning like Dorothy's courtroom advocate, the puzzled Straw Man asks, "Then why didn't you tell her before?" Here's the Good Witch's whopper: "Because she wouldn't have believed me." Not true. Dorothy believes everything. She is an exemplar of the trusting writer— the writer who must follow her imagination's whims wherever they take her, who lets herself believe whatever her imagination tells her.

If Rushdie is right, Dorothy is a magical being who not only rode the tornado but created it. And if Aunt Em is right, and what Dorothy confronted is "all in her head," then what a sublime head Dorothy has, and what visions she has conjured to transfigure her narrow, dust-blown world.

Food & Sex: How to Overcome Their Inherent Boringness

I am the daughter of a hospital cook. If you've experienced much hospital cooking, please don't hold that against my mother or me. As a cook she had one day off each week. Otherwise she was up at five a.m. to head for work. For twenty-three years she worked as a cook, with a seventeen-mile drive to work each way. And when finally she retired, she lacked ten cents of making five dollars an hour. I can't begin to tell you how much I admired her. To give you a sense of the sort of woman she was, here's a story.

When she was first married, she and my father raised chickens. One day she drove into the driveway and saw chickens staggering, their wattles all white. And then she saw something that struck her with horror: a weasel sucking blood from under a chicken's wing. She ran out of the car, took off one of her high heels, beat the weasel off the chicken with her heel, saved the chicken, and at last gained the respect of her in-laws.

My mother cooked very early, as a young child. I too cooked—not as early as she did, but I cooked dinners regularly before I was fourteen. I will confess, I cooked with irritation bordering on rage. Cooking was, for me, so representative of the more tedious aspects of necessity that at last I forced myself to experiment as a way to survive. I made meatloaves of my own invention: meatloaves with cheese inside, meatloaves with mashed potatoes inside, meatloaves with peppers inside, meatloaves with meatloaves inside.

It would take reading M. F. K. Fisher, years later, for me to begin to appreciate how food could be made interesting. What Fisher did was to bring her obsessions with food into literature—to make food into a narrative, and to make narrative into something like food.

This may be hard to believe, but there was a time when braising wasn't always written about as if it led to enlightenment. Once upon a time, food was not a subject dwelt upon in so very many books, so very rapturously. M.F. K. Fisher was one of the authors who changed that—and who discovered how to write about the subject of food without actually having been born French.

Fisher sexualized stomach hunger and, in doing so, wrote about what frequently seems inert—food—in ways that made her subject volcanic. Perhaps one day we'll have great writers of decoupage, crochet, and wood burning, but it seems that writing about fulfilling the appetites offers distinct advantages over writing about many other human activities. A magical transformation occurs. A narrative is involved, whereby food is transformed, becoming us.

If we're successful as cooks, we don't see our creations for long. If we're successful as animals, we don't see food in front of us for long either. There's the pie. Now it's gone. Where can it be? Apparently I ate it. That simple fact—eating is the act of making a substance disappear, of internalizing the external—comes alive for Fisher. A meal, like plot in fiction as described by the novelist Walter Mosley, turns into a "structure of revelations."

What Fisher calls her major symbol, her generative device—hunger—is a metaphor of return. Hunger is the guest that always comes back. And while a good meal is like a departure when it surprises us, a good meal may also be a marvelously fulfilled expectation. The poet Robert Hass testifies to the peculiarly satisfying quality of repeating an experience:

> Though predictable is an ugly little word in daily life, in our first experience of it we are clued to the hope of a shapeliness in things. To see that power working on adults, you have to catch them out: the look of foolish happiness on the faces of people who have just sat down to dinner is their knowledge that dinner will be served.

Let me tell you a story that has nothing to do—you'll see why—

with eating. It's a story about sea monkeys. If you have never suc-
cumbed to the glamour of sea monkeys, I can't say I pity you. Sea
monkeys are relatives of brine shrimp. They're so small they're al-
most invisible. After we bought a packet of sea monkeys, my younger
daughter and I started our little colony in an old mason jar filled with
water. In a couple of weeks we had the most wonderful sea monkeys.
We didn't even need to use a magnifying glass to see them. We held
the jar close to our eyes and watched the sea monkeys wheeling about.
This was very exciting. Too exciting.

I was afraid the sea monkeys would get bored, and so I decided
to give them the most beautiful new home. I ordered the "executive"
sea monkey set—with a gold rim, a statue of a crowned sea monkey,
magnified viewing port holes. My daughter and I followed all direc-
tions. We carefully transferred our sea monkeys from their old mason
jar into their deluxe executive accommodations. A few days later my
daughter cried out, "Mom, where are the sea monkeys?"

They were dead.

If you are the caretaker of a thriving sea monkey colony, you
probably have advice for me. But my point here isn't about sea mon-
keys but about the value of simplicity.

I should have listened to those sea monkeys. They were doing fine
in their mason jar.

Why am I writing about this? I want to underscore how mercifully
clear Fisher can be in her injunctions. "The best way to eat is simply,
without affectation and adulteration," she argues. I'm refreshed and
reassured to think how basic her recipes are. Not all, of course. She
has at least one recipe that calls for a calf's head. Yet she was able to
appreciate not only the most complex meals but the most simple.
And she was able to write in a direct, frank way that continues to keep
her prose alive for us.

There's a pose that M.F. K. Fisher adopts in casual photos at
virtually every stage of her life. She can be sitting in a chair or lying

on the ground, but her hands are behind her head. It's the universal pose of luxuriating, undefended, unguarded. She seems to be breathing in everything around her. Of course, writing can't be done in that particular posture, but the incubation, the gestation of writing can be. When Fisher wrote, she translated and renewed experience, using words not only to awaken the senses but to make us experience words themselves as sensuous.

Recently I heard a fiction writer declare before an audience that writing is not a generally sensual activity. He argued that we tend to move immediately from word to concept. My own experience and, I suspect, Fisher's, is quite different. Her writing conjures not only sound but color and even tactile sensations. She may loll around in photographs but her food doesn't, nor do the words she uses. A confectionary replica of the cathedral of Milano becomes "a flag flying for the chef, a bulwark all in spun sugar against the breath of corruption." Tea is "strong enough to trot a mouse on." Beer "explodes." "Peaches [shine] like translucent stained glass," and "a big tureen of hot borsht" is capable of "blasting ... safe tidy little lives." For all her delicacy of feeling, Fisher confesses to possessing an outrageous appetite. She coins a phrase for her youthful ability to eat: "husky gutted." She notes falling into a "digestive coma." She also recognized capacities for outsized enjoyment in others. A Burgundian woman is "almost fanatical about food like a medieval woman possessed by the devil." Another woman eats so much "she was like a squirrel, with hidden pouches."

In her last years, brutalized by Parkinson's and arthritis and unable to use her fingers to write, her voice reduced to a whisper, Fisher worked with a tape recorder and an assistant, continuing in her ambition to express heightened experience. When she wrote of food, as she told interviewers and claimed often in her prose, she wrote of love—and of what she called the hunger for love. Her capacity for love was also a capacity to endure the inevitable suffering that attends the loss of those we love. But it is most important to recall that she was one of the writers on the side of happiness. Our store of happiness is always in danger of being depleted. Fisher remains one of the replenishing artists.

PURITY

It's Such a Filthy Word

Look up *purity* in an Internet search engine, and you're likely to be brought to popular questionnaires that purportedly determine your level of incorruption. One set of purity-test options spans a spectrum from "had a date" to "committed bestiality." Another ranges from "kissed someone" to "had sex on the astral or ethereal planes." Either way, in these schemes we end up with the non-human. That's one of the less dangerous destinations to which purity seems to lead.

"Pure? What does it mean?"

Sylvia Plath asks the question in "Fever 103" and creates a spectacle, an outrageous hallucinatory reverie that extricates her speaker from past identities: "I am too pure for you or anyone." This is an ascent, not an answer. In "Lady Lazarus" the purifying rays of rage overwhelm as well. "I rise with my red hair / And I eat men like air." Pure? To paradise Plath's speaker goes—where only the pure thrive. We can applaud Plath's satire, well knowing that it is foolish to think we are beyond the absolutism of purity. Billions of advertising dollars prove otherwise in attempts to repel or disguise age and imperfection. And the fanaticism that breathes down the necks of many people often derives its power from conceptions of purity.

We know that the rhetoric of purity can be connected to horrific violence, ethnic "cleansing," theories of supremacy in race and religious sect, and violence against women, all seemingly ancient in the equation they make between "purity" and the honor of the group. One of the most contradictory and appalling phrases: *Honor killing.* The terrible history of purity goes on.

Elizabeth Taylor Takes a Bath

How do we conceptualize purity? What can we make purity mean? Simplicity? Innocence? Does purity exist as a relic in the mind? Is purity the devil's hot white hell and desert landscape and rock garden?

There are some rational answers: Purity can be conceptualized as positive, certainly, if we're talking about food safety, but often the concept in action refers to destruction (cleansing, scouring, eliminating); or to paralysis (unchanging, outside time); or to exclusion, as a principle of judgment ordained by an intolerant God. If we say "That's pure poetry," we're engaging in a cliché. If we say "That's pure fiction," we're engaging in an insult. We don't often use the phrase "a clean mind." The more popular phrase is "a dirty mind." We speak of a "spotless" reputation. Of course reputation can't be controlled. There is, after all, the Internet.

Even the age of innocence is getting a shorter life cycle. It's not at all surprising to hear that children are exposed to explicit language through various media, but it can be revelatory to encounter the results of that exposure firsthand. I was outside the local middle school waiting for my younger daughter to emerge at the end of the school day. As I stood with other parents I overheard a group of fifth-graders talking. The graphic specificity of those children's accumulating obscenities was astonishing. I felt like saying, "Please. There are adults present."

Purity is a subject, surely one of the great subjects, and one of the inescapable literary subjects. Much literature has been made of purity threatened, violated, and bloodied. In *The Odyssey* the handmaids disloyal to Penelope are murdered. But first, in a command that's haunting for its cruelty, they're put to work sponging away the blood of the men they slept with, men slaughtered by Odysseus. *Tess of the d'Urbervilles* was first subtitled *A Pure Woman Faithfully Presented.* Pure-hearted, desperate Tess is betrayed not only by the incredible violence she endures, but by cultural conceptions of women's sexuality that she has herself internalized. Her guilt for murder is betrayed by a bloodstain seeping through the ceiling.

Purity can be either the angel of inspiration or its assassin. As cultural conception and resonant subject matter, purity may be experienced as an imaginative pull, a drawing force with its own enigmatic power. And yet in the process of making art, an idealization of purity may become a bitter antagonist, sternly disallowing much of what is muddled, snarled, and anarchic about being human. Purity can even be an outcome of ambition gone wrong, causing sterility or over-refinement, a self-rejection on the writer's part that bleaches originality from the work.

Of course absolute purity is unattainable and thus belongs to the country of the imagination. But so much depends on the quality of the imagination.

§

The great defense against purity in art belongs to Pablo Neruda. In "Some Thoughts on Impure Poetry," he advocates

> A poetry as impure as a suit or a body, a poetry stained by food and shame, a poetry with wrinkles, observations, dreams, waking, prophecies, declarations of love and hatred, beasts, blows, idylls, manifestos, denials, doubts, affirmations, taxes.

He concludes his impassioned defense: "He who would flee from bad taste is riding for a fall." It may seem easy to argue for impurity now that Pablo Neruda has done it for us, but purity raises its stern face, its call for an uncorrupt beauty, and more. Its meanings accumulate.

Is purity Wallace Stevens's "Nothing that is not there and the nothing that is" from "The Snow Man," or Blake's "Little Lamb"? Or readiness for divine inspection, as in "Cleanness" from the Middle English Pearl Poet:

> Be careful, in coming, that thy robes be clean
> and decent for the holy-day, lest thou meet with harm;
> if thou approach that Prince of noble peerage,
> he hates hell no more than men who are soiled.

Or consider Charles Lamb's "Cleanliness" in which "Virtue [is] next to Godliness." Not only that, but

> Soil deliberate to endure,
> On the skin to fix a stain
> Till it works into the grain,
> Argues a degenerate mind,
> Sordid, slothful, ill inclin'd,
> Wanting in that self-respect
> Which does virtue best protect.

Or is the urge toward purity captured by James Fenton in "The Gene-Pool" from *Out of Danger?*

> You are unclean!
> Get out! Get out!
> Out of the gene-pool, Gene.

ξ

Lives, including literary lives, may be led in pursuit of the phantom of purity. A study of that phantom, even in its minor dimensions, can create literature. In her short story "You Should Have Seen the Mess," Muriel Spark gives us the point of view of a seventeen-year-old who forsakes all other values but cleanliness, rejecting even a generous, kind, and handsome young man because of the condition of his linens. This hygienic, self-satisfied little person seems perfectly comfortable and benignly confident about her choices. She's clean, and she's stupid.

ξ

Purity? What does it mean—as long as we have memories? Memory itself may be both spotty and spotted. It's hard to believe that any adult's past can be pure in any of the senses in which the concept of purity has been thought to reside. Unless I'm mis-remembering, it's recorded somewhere that Elizabeth Taylor said that she felt her virginity was restored after every hot bath. She forgot to add that it takes not only a bath, but a bad memory and a miracle. Of course a renunciation of the past, a purging of our rumpled and bedraggled histories, means that our ability to remember has to be degraded: Stuck a feather in his hat and called it—some kind of noodle.

In much literature, purity is both a necessary impulse and a dangerous aspiration. The compulsion to purify is part of the literary instinct, its compacting, its extremes of selection, the prominence of the "telling detail," even the commonly held ideal that the work should foster an illusion of inevitability from which no extraneous matter diverts us. The pressure to purify, to honor silence—to cut the line, the stanza, the sentence—can be a primary drive. And yet we can never be or make the ultimately pure, and so the attempt may bear the mark of both ambition and rejection, including self-rejection. On the path toward a new voice, we fall into the ditch of wordlessness again.

Poets in particular are tempted to edit the past, expunging youthful errors or exuberances or indulgences, even those marks of individuality that amount to originality. Of all literary forms, the poem, brought up on the most often declared need for concision of any verbal art form, is endangered by the poet's proclivity toward whittling until the poem is whittled out of existence. Mallarmé sought to "purify the language of the tribe," and Pound, who admired the fascist "purifier" Mussolini, echoed him. The language assigned to purity can exalt or condemn—or collapse the pillars of the creative act in retrospect. Marianne Moore's most famous excisions were in her poem "Poetry," paring that trademark piece from just shy of thirty lines to a total of three, until the opening "I, too, dislike it" takes on even greater weight, given that the illustrative material is stripped away and a knowledgeable reader must note the loss of hands, eyes, hair, a bat, elephants, a horse, a wolf, a tree, a critic, a flea, a sports fan, a statistician, "'business documents and / school-books,'" "half poets," poets, gardens, toads, and "raw material."

When I was an eleven-year-old obsessed with poetry I confessed as much to a quick-sketch cartoon artist at the Free Fair in Ionia, Michigan. He drew my picture atop a tower of books. My legs became little dangly babyish things draped over the top couple of books, the name "Shakespeare" jotted on the spine of a thick volume. Those legs were such an embarrassment to me, suggesting powerlessness and yet vanity and presumption where they dangled. My great pure dream had been reduced to comedy and hopelessness. Well, that's adolescence. Or pre-adolescence. Or adulthood. We are vast to ourselves, but miniature to others.

Sometimes the urge to purify takes a truly destructive turn. Writers who want to purify their work may ultimately want to purify the world of their work. Emily Dickinson requested that her writing be burned. Hawthorne asked that his drafts of unfinished work be destroyed. Patrick White claimed that he destroyed his drafts, but according to his biographer David Marr in the *Sydney Morning Herald*, the reality was otherwise: "The old bastard. Patrick White told the world over and over that none of this existed. 'Don't bother hunting for drafts and manuscripts,' he snapped when I asked him years ago. 'They've all gone into the pit.'" According to Marr, the drafts were "stuffed into cupboards and drawers in [White's] house on the edge of Centennial Park." Others who talked about wanting their papers tossed into the flames include Thomas Hardy, Vladimir Nabokov, and Philip Larkin. The connection between the corporeal body and the corpus of manuscripts is undeniable. The phenomenon may remind us of Oscar Wilde's putative last words, "Either that wallpaper goes, or I do." As fate would have it, the author always goes, but not always the paper.

Purity Is Perfection's Mother

In 2006 Helen Vendler visited the subject of the destruction of drafts in her criticism of Alice Quinn's edition of Elizabeth Bishop's uncollected poems and drafts, *Edgar Allan Poe & the Juke-Box*, accusing Quinn, according to the *New York Times Book Review*, "of undermining Bishop's legacy and of betraying something sacred, the poet's personal trust." Vendler is quoted as saying, "If you make people promise to burn your manuscripts they should," and arguing that "personal fidelity is more important than art." She used as one of her examples the supposed request of Virgil to have his writings burned. Whatever our opinion, on the matter of Bishop, are we betraying Virgil at this moment by calling to mind the *Aeneid?* Legendary last wishes aim for the ultimate purification. Nothing is more pure than nothingness. Nothing is more perfect than nothing.

A "rabbit catcher" is an old term for a midwife. Plath has a poem by that name that's about an actual snare as well as a psychological snare. But it wasn't rabbits she was catching. In the famous foreword to *Ariel*, Robert Lowell narrates a metamorphosis of Plath into a heightened inhuman purity: she "becomes herself, becomes something imaginary, newly, wildly and subtly created—hardly a person at all, or a woman, certainly not another 'poetess,' but one of those super-real, hypnotic, great classical heroines." Lowell tells us that we hear "the pounding pistons of her heart." Plath, he says, is "machinelike from hard training," with "her hand of metal with its modest, womanish touch." The modest touch of the hand that wrote "Daddy"? Lowell's introduction to *Ariel* contains one of the most painful lines in any literary appraisal: "This poetry and life are not a career; they tell that life, even when disciplined, is simply not worth it."

To a machine, no. To an absolutist of the purest sort, no. But then succumbing to purity is what Plath is refusing to do in some of her last work. When she turned and looked purity in the face she wrote the poems that made her name. She chose a subject—purity—that could disable as much as liberate her gift. For the artist, a preoccupation with artistic purity can be death to amplitude and instinct, and an enemy of generativity. It stops us. If she seemed more "super-real" and "machine-like" to Lowell, to other readers Plath's speakers in some of her final poems are more humanly complex.

If once I thought that perfection was the mother of purity I have only recently realized that I had the generations wrong. Purity is older; purity is perfection's mother. Purity looks backward, to a prior state of being that was whole, unsophisticated, unadulterated. Perfection, like most children, is not interested in the past as much as in the future. However unattainable, it is perfection, not purity, that harbors the notion of achievement after an apprenticeship. Perfection claims action for itself, whereas purity is a state of being, not an action. Once lost, purity may not be regained or sought in the same site. Purity, more elemental than perfection, takes its metaphorical weight from our perceptions of the body and what the body can bear.

Both purity and perfection are allied conceptions, but purity is the more dangerous. Not least of all because we so seldom think about what purity might actually mean. More often we simply react, repelled at some level by an insufficiency that appears to be beyond imperfect, that attacks our sense of wholesome physical integrity.

§

After my first daughter was born I experienced months in which I felt one-dimensional. How could I make the world orderly and safe enough for a vulnerable baby? What was pure enough for my daughter? I admit that I come from a family where the failure to clean out thoroughly a can of tuna fish was held in the same contempt reserved in other families for a member convicted of forging checks.

Becoming a mother was such a dramatic transformation and so resistant to my usual descriptive resources that I felt keenly that my language couldn't keep up with my circumstances. My resistance to previous shapes I had made in poetry was severe. I endured a tightening of possibilities. Who was this imperfect stranger I was? A loathsome purity came over me. The spaces in my work became more prominent, as phrases pulled back upon themselves. I neglected to respect the vitality of the vernacular. I pared away draft after draft. Only gradually did I re-learn how to allow more life into my writing—that is, more of language, graced with its inevitable impurities.

Before I stopped trying to purify my writing as a new mother, I was treating my poems like the ancient Greeks treated women, in Anne Carson's interpretation.

In "Dirt and Desire: Essay on the Phenomenology of Female Pollution in Antiquity," Carson quotes Hesiod: "Let a man not clean his skin in water that a woman has washed in. For a hard penalty follows on that for a long time." The Greek obsession with boundaries focuses on women, Carson informs us:

> Women, then, are pollutable, polluted and polluting in several ways at once. They are anomalous members of the human class, being, as Aristotle puts it, imperfect men ... They are, as social entities, units of danger, moving across boundaries of family and house, in marriage, prostitution, or adultery. They are, as psychological entities, unstable compounds of deceit and desire, prone to leakage.

Whether limning Sappho's fragments or writing her own poems, Carson troubles boundaries, puncturing but also illuminating pure form. Carson's poetry achieved recognition precisely because of its resistance to genre purity and exclusivity, for its cross-breeding of scholarship and the lyric and for its heightened attention to purity, silence, and abjection. As she writes of Sappho's transgressive poems, it is the image of "an irony of reference as sharp as a ray of light" that she chooses to employ, even while she breaks the bulwarks between classical scholarship and lyric poetry.

In "The Glass Essay" Carson writes of an abjection that mixes human and animal categories, taking the romantic poem of longing in a direction that assails purity:

Everything I know about love and its necessities
I learned in that one moment
when I found myself
thrusting my little burning red backside like a baboon
at a man who no longer cherished me.

I can recall a performance by Laurie Anderson during which she quoted the above lines from Carson's poem. A gasp went through even that seldom-shocked audience.

Deflowering

Which brings me to Plath again. Carson's baboon image opposes the organic metaphor that has most closely followed women, in multiple cultures: the flower. The flower in its symbolic context establishes an equation: flower, woman, poet—ethereal and fleeting, fragile and lovely and pure. No baboon there. For Carson's image to strike we have to bring with us a conception of women and purity that may seem retrograde. Change the genders and the baboon image performs in a wholly different way.

In a well-known photograph of Plath, a hand reaches toward her with a carnation while Plath's own fingers linger on her scarf. She is looking up, in the other direction from the flower, her mouth open in a smile only partly realized. In another photograph, from 1953, Plath is holding a rose upside down and smiling as if in parody of the role she is supposed to be playing as "female poet." The sexual politics of that literary period suggested that the female of a certain class was somehow exalted but embarrassing. As was women's poetry. It is no accident that much of the drama of Plath's novel *The Bell Jar* is about reproduction and the control of reproduction, the "deflowering" of the protagonist. Once "deflowered," Esther Greenwood can't stop bleeding and must be exposed, her privacy violated, her interior broached not only in private but within the medical establishment.

In the lower left of the famous daguerreotype of Emily Dickinson a flower may go almost unnoticed. The blossom between Dickinson's fingers seems like an ornament, a blurry sign, a bow to convention more than a physical reminder of Dickinson's disciplined attention to her conservatory. And the book on the table next to her—is that a prop, too? (We might have more images of Dickinson if she had enjoyed having her image captured.) Flowers can be seen as purifiers in the way they have been deployed, whether the flowers are turned from lightly as in Plath's photographs or presented in Dickinson's daguerreotype frontally and yet overwhelmed by her steady human gaze.

That there is something "pure" about Dickinson's gaze in the daguerreotype is undeniable, it seems to me. She looks out of time and beyond time, and like other writers working with restraining structures (has ever the simplest hymnal form been employed more stubbornly, for such radical advances?) she is imparting the lessons an only part-time purist is capable of teaching. We go to Dickinson for a sensibility that detonates upon close examination and for breath work of the subtlest kind. We go to Virginia Woolf to trace a style that illuminates consciousness as it moves about an absence. We go to Plath to scour the image clean in one tributary of her ambition. We go to Plath, too, to put the dagger in the heart, to understand *Listen, bastards, she's through.*

And wasn't Hemingway a purist? It was a strange experience for me to read his fiction after a friend pointed out how often Hemingway uses the word *and.* Shouldn't such a word suggest inclusiveness, a non-hierarchical in-gathering—isn't that a possible reading? Except that the coordinating conjunction is surrounded by the pressure of silence, by the untouched and unreal, the wound that can't show itself, the wound of the perfect man who must insinuate more than sully the moment of grace with ungraceful speech. Or think of Anita

Brookner, with her repetitive plots, milling the same sorts of characters in the same quietly devastating situations, creating a literature as intricate and beautiful and pure in some ways as Matisse's palm fronds (as depicted by Elaine Scarry).

There is a possibility of reckoning with the impulse to purify without being damaged in the attempt. And if there is at least a family connection between perfection and purity, a visual artist helps us.

The painter Agnes Martin, 1912–2004, born in Saskatchewan, is known for her grid-like paintings, composed like the most minute acts of attention, purposefully just shy of perfection. Not that she sought perfection in substance or execution. She sought the idea of perfection as stimulus: "I hope I have made it clear that the work is *about* perfection as we are aware of it in our minds but that the paintings are very far from being perfect—completely removed in fact—even as we ourselves are." Or, as she explains, "you get light enough and you levitate." Her canvases resemble landing directions, fields that point toward a clarified state of mind. Her lines and shadings prompt a recalibration and refreshment of sight. Her pale washes of colors, her obligingly imperfect lines, make the purity of calmness and silence and emptiness palpable.

And yet, at first sight her canvases are, frankly, easy to ignore. They arrive in low-intensity, until we adjust and turn up our own intensity. I am fond of *Untitled No. 1*, "acrylic and graphite on canvas" (1993), with its eggshell tint so faint that the canvas makes me think of a Platonic archetype of paper. Other titles emerge as pre-Oedipal, suggesting feeling states before language: *Infant Response to Love, I Love the Whole World, Happiness—Glee, Little Children Playing with Love.* The works are like surfaces still to be written on, and yet are curiously inviolable. Many look like unassuming writing tablets, the kind we used when we were children, the horizontal lines allowing us to form our first letters according to a template of perfection that we were meant to absorb. Indeed, Martin is the artist of the fresh-lined page, the page that is already art before we make our first mark. As she has written, "Seeking awareness of perfection in the mind is called living the inner life. It is not necessary for artists to live the inner life. It is only necessary for them to recognize inspiration or to represent it."

Inspiration is difficult to represent, but to beg the question, difficulty is an artist's inspiration. Nothing is more difficult than perfection, except for purity. I turn to Gerard Manley Hopkins to see such inspiration at work as he describes purity as if it were renewable perfection. He writes in "God's Grandeur," "There lives the dearest freshness deep down things." The freshness is dear. The freshness is deep. Such deep purity, in the same poem, lives with these lines:

> And all is seared with trade; bleared, smeared with toil;
> And wears man's smudge and shares man's smell: the soil
> Is bare now, nor can foot feel, being shod.

The poem is from 1877. At the time, Hopkins could say in the same poem—with confidence, as we cannot—"nature is never spent."

ξ

Pure? What does it mean? Plath was right, perhaps, not to answer, but instead to demonstrate how it feels to be overwhelmed by an ideology of purity and then to be spurred into impure voice, acknowledging the power of purity as a cultural preoccupation. When Neruda assails purity he ends with a threat to those who are overcome, raging in his defense of impurity because he knows purity's power, a power that even he, wily and defiant, could not ignore.

Wrestling with the conception of purity, James Fenton writes in more abstract terms in an untitled poem, "This is no time for people who say: this, this, and only / this. We say: this, and *this,* and *that* too." Purity is not human, nor is perfection, but both, we should keep reminding ourselves, are inventions of the human imagination at its most ambitious. The products of the imagination demand their own life.

Czesław Miłosz in *Unattainable Earth* knowingly or not echoes Neruda when he tells us that the new poetry will include both "the rhythm of the body ... heartbeat, pulse, sweating ... together with the sublime needs of the spirit, and our duality will find its form in [the new poetry], without renouncing one zone or the other."

Purity will take its place. We can't help but be disappointed if we long after purity in art or in life. But then, a great amount of literature, inevitably, must be made out of disappointment.

Bigamy for Beginners

Audacious Ambition: Writing Across Genres

Writing across genres can be a sign of bloated ambition, misapplied ambition, or even a product of ambition avoided, a deliberate dodge to escape even a modicum of near-mastery of techniques within a single genre. But writing across the major genres can also be a sign that a writing life may require more apertures, more outlets, and that for some writers the most fruitful ambition can best be realized on multiple fronts.

In other words, if you're writing in more than one genre you may not be misaligning your talent so much as acknowledging that you're voracious and that your appetite for writing requires variety.

Whatever the case, a writer must face the difficulties of working across genres, difficulties that emerge not only from readers or publishers, but from within the genres themselves.

ξ

The poet who turns to screenwriting. The novelist who writes poetry. The playwright who composes short stories. The critic who is plotting a novel. Admit it: Doesn't a certain suspicion attach to each? As if to cross over from a primary genre into another genre is like cheating on one's true love. Or like bigamy. Or like the creep wearing a smoking jacket in a detective novel who lures the innocent maid to his bed. The second genre is the illicit liaison. Something on the side.

Even if it's not viewed as cheating, to write in more than one major genre (poetry, fiction, plays, screenplays, and their variants) can be seen as grubbing about. You might be a perpetual neophyte in the second genre. Not only announcing yourself as a start-up, but enduring condescension from long-practiced writers of the invaded genre. Because any art is hard. Until you've soaked in the genre and written far beyond your first endorphin-inspired juvenilia and crashed on the rocks of frustration, who do you think you are? And won't you, upon meeting inevitable frustration in the new genre, gather yourself up and trudge across the shore to yet another genre, at best attaining only a pinch worth of competence?

What if a writer becomes the jack-of-all-trades and the master of none? How can any multi-genre writer even answer that legitimate question? There's always recourse to Walt Whitman, who composed at least one line that could be a stock answer for those who can't resist crossing genres: "I am large, I contain multitudes." Besides which, he had the good sense to write his own reviews.

Then again, we can think of the honorable example of John Updike. Martin Amis wrote of that man of letters:

> He said he had four studies in his house so we can imagine him writing a poem in one of his studies before breakfast, then in the next study writing a hundred pages of a novel, then in the afternoon he writes a long and brilliant essay for the *New Yorker*, and then in the fourth study he blurts out a couple of poems.

What Amis admired was not only Updike's apparent ease and speed, but the span of his ambitions across genres.

Where Is the Letter *B*?

Why consider genres at all? Genres are bundled conventions that may shift or expand or retract. And something always escapes categorization. Yet outliers may exert magnetic force and grow up to inspire genres of their own. For my part, I've found that arguments against registering distinctions among major writing genres (poetry, drama, short stories, the novel, the novella) are likely to come from people who can specify the precise attributes of a bewildering number of signature beers. What goes unacknowledged by those who resist recognizing the distinctive power of each major genre is how resistant the imagination can be to manipulation, how conventions can more readily be parodied than sincerely deployed and sustained in a piece of writing, how choosing to write in a genre presents a series of affronts to previous technique and conviction, and a stand-in-the-wind repudiation of the threat of meaninglessness. Writing in any genre is a matter of exposure to that genre and the ability to integrate that genre's conventions, especially if one wishes to claim distinctiveness in the genre, including distinctiveness attained through subversion.

Genres are embedded with remarkably complex techniques primed by assumptions that have developed over particular historical periods. As such, genres bear within them accumulated tensions that school their practitioners and that create predictable and unpredictable effects, given different contexts and different audiences. The pleasure of breaking style or breaking out of genre or blending or warping generic conventions lies in the realization of the events that transpire in the act of summoning the genre's leading features—as an opportunity. Genres and subgenres create conditions for writing, and we find ourselves responding to them and sometimes experiencing a mysterious affinity.

That is, immersion in a genre is more like love than we may be ready to admit.

Any genre has enough challenges for infinite lifetimes, so why engage in more than one? To engage in a genre seriously means that investments in reading and listening and practicing must accrue until, if we're fortunate and passionately disciplined (or disciplined by passion), a template is established, an internal organizing system, largely beyond awareness, in which intuitions in language can be captured.

A very simple example: Some of us, particularly those who have had bad secretarial jobs, are quick typists. But if asked to draw the keypad we would be at a loss. Where is the letter *B?* The template for writing within a genre is like that—a way of implicitly organizing a response. A template exists not only to allow us to deploy convention but to withstand convention.

So much, however, depends on the territory one decides to experiment upon. An old argument exists that there is no sense in defining genres, given the permeability of language and given that genres are dependent on readers' expectations and thus are in flux. Admittedly, some genres are more multiply implicated in other genres. Especially if you happen to be a novelist, you are already often a multi-genre worker. If the novel is still a "loose baggy monster," as Henry James complained of the nineteenth-century novel, the baggy pants contain so much patchwork material from other reference areas that to write a novel is to engage in practices that are anything but genre-tight. The novel stuffs into its pockets all it can: letters, poetry, ledgers, emoticons.

In some cases a writer may be working in a primary genre but recognizes the work as spanning another genre. Muriel Spark always considered herself a poet and her novels a species of poetry. Elizabeth Bishop's letters were posthumously gathered in a volume titled *One Art,* as if the genres of poetry and letter writing are hardly separable. Marianne Moore was never entirely comfortable calling what she made *poems,* and it is doubtful that she was the only writer questioning how to categorize aesthetic efforts. Perhaps many of us feel akin to the character in the V. S. Naipaul story, a carpenter who is happiest when making, and failing to finish, what he called (and what Naipaul's story is called) "The Thing Without a Name." Yet all writing depends on generating conventions that are dominant in some genres more than in others and on satisfying or subverting or reorienting readers' expectations. Genres make different demands on writers—which is one of the reasons why one genre may be so supremely attractive to some writers and so off-putting to others.

My sense of the not-always-yielding boundaries of genres comes from my experience of the sheer difficulty of moving between major genres, the way genres seem to come with a rind or a negative charge, repulsing advances. Poets in particular may face a heated challenge when writing prose, particularly fiction. "My Life had stood—a Loaded Gun—," to quote Emily Dickinson. So had her art, that loaded gun. For a poet, working in another genre can seem like leaving the gun out on the counter, unattended.

The transition from one genre to another means reversing habits and setting up a new relationship with both time and space on the page. In its many incarnations, not only through indebtedness to the Romantics, poetry tends to rely on compression and thus on intense concentration on both the reader and the writer's part. In *The Poem's Heartbeat* Alfred Corn advises writers to recognize whether they are poets or prose writers by asking themselves: "'Am I interested in conveying a truth that is broad and seamless as a mural or tapestry or am I interested in conveying a vision that is really a series of intuitive and technical lightning flashes?' If the latter description of the writer's task is the one that most attracts you, then poetry is the better fit."

A truth? Or a vision? Or both? Or could the terms be reversed? The prose writer is more interested in the vision, the poet in the truth? What seems to hold up best in Corn's inspired metaphor, however, is the way creation is apprehended. The broad versus the flashing. I associate lyric poetry with a certain receptiveness, the work of waiting for the right alignment when the boat of language (or skiff or cruise ship or tanker) crests up against imaginative experience. I hope to come closer to both actuality and the unreal, to an aspect of my instinctive nature or an alignment of conceptions that lurks off my usual map of comprehension.

Provocatively, Cynthia Ozick argues that poets cannot successfully make a transition into writing fiction, whereas serious writers always have done field work in poetry: "Writers who are artists either write poetry or have written poetry, but I don't think poets can be fiction writers. The novels written by poets are often not true novels; they are long, long poems." I hope Ozick is wrong, and yet I have to admit that writing fiction seriously, regularly, with increasing ambition, posed two particular problems for me.

First, movement. Which is ironic, given that, as we're told repeatedly in virtually any context where the term appears, *verse* itself means "to turn"—designating motion, a doubling-back upon language. And yet, if you're a poet with my tendencies, try getting a fictional character to dislodge herself from a table and step over to a window. There are so many ways to do this, and each seems like a revelation. You can even refuse (often the best choice) to show the character in transit. But here's the trouble, at least the trouble that used to emerge for me: In poetry I'm propelled by a rhythm that is so dominant that new combinations appear dictated by the aural. In fiction a rhythmic charge is at work, but aural effects don't initially guide me as emphatically as they do when I'm writing poetry.

Fiction is a rather sneaky art—at least the kind that I want to write. Even Nabokov's *Lolita,* for all its lush wordplay, becomes devastating gradually. It is poetic prose, but it is still prose.

In turning to fiction, the second difficulty, I find, involves working with cause and effect. In much fiction, particularly fiction that adopts at least some of the conventions of realism, effects have causes that are discernible. A plot is a chain of them. Of course cause and effect can be evaded. Consider Gertrude Stein—who wrote, by the way, in more than one genre. But the way I work with time in short stories or longer fiction differs from the way I experience time in my poetry, where simultaneous events more often occur. The sense of daily life in my own fiction is meant to convey a realist illusion that leads toward culmination in particular places and across time, where consequences matter. I hope in fiction to create compassion for an ensemble of characters in their dailiness and—sometimes—to create an illusion of reality interrupted by the miraculous.

Art Is Long and Life Is Shorter and Shorter

Even when writers have made discoveries by crossing the borders of the conventionally agreed-upon major genres, their reputations (determined in part by academia and the marketing categories of publishers and retail booksellers) tend to be housed within one genre. This happens even to the most extraordinary writers. Shakespeare is linked to his plays more often than to his sonnets. Thomas Hardy divided his life between fiction and poetry, returning fully to poetry in his later career, although his reputation as a poet lags, unfortunately, behind his reputation as a novelist. The major modernists wrote as a matter of course in multiple genres, but are more often remembered for work in a single genre. We think less often of T. S. Eliot's criticism and drama; Ezra Pound's scholarship; D. H. Lawrence's polemics, poetry, and visual art. Hilda Doolittle (H.D.) was a novelist as well as a poet. William Carlos Williams and Langston Hughes were prolific in a dizzying number of genres, including fiction, the essay, and autobiography as well as poetry.

Kingsley Amis was both a poet and a fiction writer, as were Stevie Smith and Robert Penn Warren. During his lifetime John Updike was known first and foremost as a fiction writer, despite his multigenre facility. Doris Lessing, a novelist, poet, memoirist, and political essayist, has made brilliant inroads into the radically estranging and critically under-appreciated subgenre of science fiction. Roberto Bolaño was a poet as well as a fiction writer. Rikki Ducornet is a fiction writer, essayist, poet, and painter. Among the most well-known novelists, Margaret Atwood and Michael Ondaatje and Joyce Carol Oates are all also poets. Yet the news that stays news with the latter three remains news about their fiction.

Is it that readers want artists to have a categorical identity? Is it a matter of branding (that repulsive term)? Writing makes possible a peculiar sense of intimacy—it's an illusion, but a powerful one. Do we want to recognize an author, somehow, through fixed genre? W. H. Auden addressed a similar issue in *The Dyer's Hand*: "In relation to a writer, most readers believe in the Double Standard: they may be unfaithful to him as often as they like, but he must never, never be unfaithful to them." Failure and—or—readers' indifference: both are possibilities for the writer working across genres.

A puzzling question follows writers: How much of originality is available to us, and should we worry about diminishing our originality and depleting our store of talent within our major genre if we traffic among genres? Cynthia Ozick addresses the problem, suggesting that originality is a resource that must be protected:

> Flaubert's comment, "Live like a bourgeois *so that* you may think like a demigod," held better when there was still a distinction between bohemianism and the bourgeois, but it still has a certain validity. It's really a question of originality. Are you thrifty with your originality, saving it for art, or do you dispose of it in daily life?

If we are supposed to be "thrifty with . . . originality," then presumably spreading it across multiple genres may potentially squander the originality meant for our primary genre. Even if talent seems limitless, energy is finite. The New Zealand fiction writer Janet Frame vividly described her art in terms of its strenuous requirements:

Writing a novel is not merely going on a shopping expedition across the border to an unreal land: it is hours and years spent in the factories, the streets, the cathedrals of the imagination, learning the unique functioning of Mirror City, its skies and space, its own planetary system.

Frame demonstrated extreme caution when she was hesitant to name the titles of her books after a young man asked for them: "My almost primitive shyness about naming prevented me from telling him." She cites her "reluctance to reduce or drain into speech the power supply of the named."

Because *ars longa vita brevis* and originality is hard to come by. And confidence shaky. The sensation of working with a new genre is like being in a plane whose engine we're uncertain about. Which was the trouble with the small plane I was on recently. From my window I could view a grill hole near the wing that looked as dusty and cobwebbed as a long-neglected chicken coop. The engine never resolved into a steady hum but gasped, as if making a sincere effort. Aircraft should not engage in matters of free will. Similarly, the choice of genre probably shouldn't seem entirely the product of free will; too much has to be absorbed for us to make the more trying efforts that success, even limited success, requires.

Again: the art so long, the life so short for moving across genres. And the examples so dispiriting. Even the most brilliant writers may fail in the effort. Think of Henry James and his play *Guy Domville* in 1895. Visualize him standing onstage to take his author's bow and enduring shrieks of contempt from the gallery. Philip Hensher imagined this, and in *The Guardian* went on to call a revival of James Joyce's *Exiles* "like most plays written by novelists, . . . a notoriously plonking effort," noting in turn the failures of Graham Greene, William Golding, Muriel Spark, and Iris Murdoch to write successful dramas. On the other hand, candidates for playwrights attempting

109

novels may fail just as often. Hensher includes Joe Orton and Tom Stoppard as exemplars. Or we might consider Picasso trying to be a poet, for which Gertrude Stein derided him, no doubt with territorial pique. Marianne Moore attempted without success to write a novel. The poet Jean Garrigue also tried and failed to write a full-scale novel—about an oculist. Sylvia Plath didn't fail in taking on a novel, but only thought she had, denigrating *The Bell Jar* nearly every chance she got. Her *pot-boiler*, she called it, preempting criticism.

It's not consoling to consider the above examples. Extraordinary artists and writers working outside their primary genres have been derided or have themselves underestimated the results of their labors. Nevertheless, we can't account for how such audacity in crossing genres might have refreshed or enriched their art in subterranean ways. Who knows what we bring back from real or supposed failures, or how such acts of daring are integrated, even if by stealth, into our lives and art?

With Whom Do You Identify? Echo? Or Narcissus?

Given the sheer difficulty, the resistance of genres to adaptation—given the suspicion or condescension that engaging in multiple genres elicits—why do so many of us range beyond genre?

It's a compulsion. But there are other explanations too: To break through the wall of hardened assumptions and habits. To avoid being like a bad translator of one's own work.

Think of Echo and Narcissus: with whom do you identify? Echo may be a more familiar type. She can only repeat what she has already heard. What an agony if we don't want to be echoes of our earlier selves. Because, as Rimbaud claimed and as everyone keeps quoting, "I is another." To translate oneself into an alien art form is a way to create the crisis of becoming something/someone else in the imagination. We may have a different personality in each genre. Czesław Miłosz suggested that we are all like apartment buildings—there are so many personalities in each of us. If that's the case, then there are studio apartments and suites and lobbies, and each interior personality may need another structure, another genre of being to be heard.

My guess is that there are more of us who write in multiple genres than acknowledge doing so, for fear of failure or the charge of defection. Some writers, too, never having given themselves permission to experiment, choose one genre too early. Later, they're trying to catch up.

Are there other reasons to transgress genre boundaries?

To emulate what one admires, whatever the genre.

To cultivate the sensation of beginning again—that exciting weird rawness of starting out.

To recognize difficulty as not only an obstacle but a lure.

To resist desperation after a plateau has been reached in one's principal art. Sometimes a problem that was intractable in one genre resolves itself while a writer is busy with another genre. The writer warps or rotates the conventions of the less-familiar genre. Or the writer recasts the question that began the search across genres.

To outwit perfectionism—the ideal that means we fail before we begin.

There is a lovely bonus: If we write in more than one genre we may be able to write for longer periods. When we're tapped out in one genre for the day we go on to another.

And here is another reason for unfaithfulness: *To cultivate a genre may be like gaining an additional sense faculty.* We probably all have friends who are more oriented by one sense than another. I am one of those people who miss seeing things. People like me have friends who say, "Did you see that man who walked by with a nail in his head?" To which I reply, "No, no I missed that." Genres demand that we use neglected faculties and orient our attention in unfamiliar ways. Writing is about concentration. Genres, as such, perform as focusing agents. Even failures in reading, let alone writing, are generally due to a lack of concentrated focus. Adam Zagajewski (translated by Clare Cava-nagh) writes wistfully, "If only we read poetry as carefully as menus in expensive restaurants ... "

Other possible reasons why writers cross genres? Because it is a new way to fail. We get so tired of the familiar ways.

The Writer as Metaphor

Which brings me to psychics.

The movement across genres is a test of the imagination and another way to tell time. And to tell about time. According to James Wood, the novelist better known as a critic, "The true writ-er, that free servant of life, is one who must always be acting as if life were a category beyond anything the novel had yet grasped." That dash to the unknown is part of the attraction of writing. Is writing in another genre a means of time travel? The psychic medium John Edward called his television program and one of his books *Crossing Over*. He manages to make some people believe he is in contact with spirits. Thinking of him and of what he must encounter, I'm reminded of what those of us who write in multiple genres face: a sense of trespass, of the unnatural, of being illegitimate. Spreading writing across genres may seem like over-reaching. And an admission of greed and colonizing tendencies. What's that in Napoleon's pocket? That's my pen.

One repercussion of such ambition may be a sense of height-ened uncertainty for the writer. How do we make illusions speak, and in what tempo? What are the conventions that animate the un-real and take on shape, while the ghost of our primary form haunts us? Does the incursion upon other genres make our primary genre more mysterious? As we establish distance by experimenting with other genres, does the original genre become more freshly intriguing? Is writing like working with phantoms? Marina Warner in *Phantasmagoria* writes of

> artists, performers, and writers ... grasping the imaginary fabric that swathes and freights our consciousness today ... They can help—and they often mean to—reorientate readers' and audiences' perceptions, and shape subjectivity within a mesh of reciprocal and social relations. Those working in this vein rough-hew inherited phantasms, not only mining their undoubted pleasure and power. In a material sense, spirits are indeed channelled, and the media are here, now.

Years ago, with a close friend, I visited a fortune-teller. The fortune-teller predicted the age at which I would die. I wish she hadn't done that. She also gave me useful advice: *Accept more invitations.* Which I did. Coincidentally, my life came to be less lonely.

I don't come from a family of gullible people, believe me, yet when she was a young woman my mother also went to a fortune-teller. Nearly everything she learned from the woman studying her tea leaves came true: the number of children she would have, and the first name of the man she would marry (which must have helped my father's chances considerably). The fortune-teller only made one gaffe. One of my mother's children, she said, would be a renowned pianist. Which meant that—despite the expense—all four of us children took piano lessons until all four of us revolted. Stupidly enough.

I've gone into this brief foray about psychics because of my sense that, like fortune-telling, our trying out a new genre may seem like an illicit adventure to those who know us primarily as one sort of writer, and also because as writers we can sometimes feel we're in contact with spirits. We call those spirits the imagination. Then, too, if we do choose to work in more than one genre we're changing our future. We're working with time in a different way, and we're engaging in the calculated risk that devoting our energy to another genre will enrich our writing life in unforeseen ways. We're changing our internal landscape, and thus our future.

There is a seldom-considered reason for writers to work in multiple genres: Moving between genres is closely allied to the most essential activity of the imagination, the metaphor. That is, crossing over genres is enacting or living out metaphor. "Metaphor is analogous to fiction," James Wood writes, "because it floats a rival reality. It is the entire imaginative process in one move." To work in multiple genres is to "float a rival reality"—to test the primary genre, perhaps, or to bring back new conceptual possibilities while in new territory. In a *Paris Review* interview, when she was asked why she writes non-fiction as well as novels, Marilynne Robinson answered:

> To change my own mind. I try to create a new vocabulary or terrain for myself, so that I open out—I always think of the Dutch claiming land from the sea—to open up something that would have been closed to me before.

The phrase "to change my own mind" becomes a literalized metaphor. Change genres = change the mind.

ξ

But then, always, we hope there will be a return. The return to the first love, the genre that made its claims on us initially. How to manage this? One writer told me that he chooses different days for different genres. *Monday: fiction. Tuesday: poetry. Wednesday: fiction. Thursday: non-fiction.* I'm reminded of day-of-the-week panties.

Writing imaginatively needs hours, hoarded time, long sinking moments. A concentration that isn't only a matter of quality but of quantity. I think of Jane Austen, working in the sitting room, subject to the sudden appearance of guests. She certainly found a way to capitalize on her situation. But it couldn't have been easy.

Some writers, like watchmakers, require the same familiar implements: tweezers, wheels, a loupe, the balance pivot, and the escape pinion. Moving into another genre requires that we recognize the implements that we've been using as writers. And the implements we rely on as readers. In particular, when exploring, I find it useful not only to be immersed in the body of work of a primary practitioner in the genre, but to read anthologies in the unfamiliar genre and a great variety of them, so that I keep freshly acquainting myself, for instance, with the implements of that genre.

Admittedly, reading a variety of selections from a variety of anthologies is a little like speed dating. You meet a lot of strangers in small doses. You don't have to marry immediately, but at the very least you do want to introduce yourself as soon as possible to those in thrall to another genre.

Once we become involved with another genre, we should hope to become more fluent, more adventurous writers. In turn, we can expect to find some of our obsessions arising again, in whatever form in which we experiment. Another personality may emerge, a different attitude, but often our obsessions are hard-wired. If you find yourself in your short stories referring repeatedly to Viking long ships and the apron your mother wore when she discovered that you'd brought home a dog, you may very well find that even if you become a playwright, somewhere in the third act, a Viking in an apron will charge the stage wielding a dog.

After a while, working steadily in another genre, there may be no turning away from that genre. You're becoming ambitious in more than one way—despite the difficulties. There you go. Gently down the stream. Or else indignantly, with great splashing, refusing to row, without a paddle.

The Selkie Returns to the Sea

Here I want to offer a caution: It's strange, that return from any other genre to a main genre. Maybe we're not unfaithful to the first, the primary genre, so much as each of us is a forager, anxious to bring back whatever we can to reinvigorate the genre that lured us to become writers in the first place.

In the legends about the selkie, her original shape, embodied in her seal skin, is hidden away by the human who loves her. Inevitably, the selkie at last discovers the bundle containing her skin and drags it from a high shelf. She can't help but put on her old skin and submerge into the waves, abandoning the human world. Yes, that happens periodically. For there is some truth to the suspicion that any art form is guarded by a jealous muse.

It's not that the skin snaps back into place after we work in other genres. The skin of any art changes shape for us perhaps, but we too have changed shape. Besides, it is the only skin we can take off and put back on again.

SECRECY

Making a Good Secret

My brother Joe was almost fifteen years older than I was, and so I missed out on his childhood. I had to learn from my mother what he was like as a young boy. She used to tell a story about how tender-hearted he was. Two of Joe's lambs died and he buried them. My mother went to see the graves. Joe had buried the lambs, all except for their faces.

When I was a child I secretly buried bracelets, necklaces, polished stones, and coins. My fantasy was that someday a child would be digging around and find what I had buried and be made wildly happy by the discovery. I buried dolls too, but I dug them up right away.

We probably never entirely grow out of burying and unburying what's valuable, and "buried secrets" is a redolent phrase with a meaning that isn't only confined to melodrama.

Like ambition, secrecy gets a bad name, and often for good reasons. Both secrecy and ambition may suggest corruption and solipsism. Both can be futile or counter-productive. Or both can be glamorous but doomed, out-Miltoning Milton and his Satan: "To reign is worth ambition, though in Hell." Ambition and secrecy are potentially self-serving, self-seeking, and self-limiting. If we combine the two words into one phrase—secret ambition—we may even hear faint mockery from the ghost of James Thurber's futile dreamer, Walter Mitty.

There are behaviors associated with either term that should be avoided.

Perhaps especially with secrecy. The least damaging associations allied to the word refer to supposed shortcuts (the secret to optimum health, the secret of attraction) and to salacious triviality (the secret lives of fetishists or exhibitionists—as these are parodied).

The more damaging connotations of secrecy include coercion,

for example the secrets of child abuse and domestic violence, and unethical institutional secrets. Secrecy is a primary property of corruption, as Sisela Bok argued decades ago:

> With no capacity for keeping secrets and for choosing when to reveal them, human beings would lose their sense of identity and every shred of autonomy ... And yet this capacity too often serves to thwart the same basic human needs, since it risks damaging the judgment and character of those who exercise it, and conceals wrongdoing of every kind.

Bok's warning continues to resonate.

In a moving reversal of the usual terms, Ha Jin in *The Writer as Migrant* makes a case for treason as a property of government rather than of individuals, taking particular note of when governments silence artists:

> Historically, it has always been the individual who is accused of betraying his country. Why shouldn't we turn the tables by accusing a country of betraying the individual? Most countries have been such habitual traitors to their citizens anyway. The worst crime the country commits against the writer is to make him unable to write with honesty and artistic integrity.

Like Ha Jin, Roberto Bolaño questions the ways in which writers are betrayed by their governments and the secrets governments keep—and how some writers may prove complicit in their own betrayal. In a narrative about governmental oppression and individual collusion, Bolaño's novel *By Night in Chile* gives us a dying priest who has been part of a literary salon that has a torture chamber in its basement. The priest struggles with his rationalizations: "One has to be responsible, as I have always said. One has a moral obligation to take responsibility for one's actions, and that includes one's words and silences, yes, one's silences, because silences rise to heaven too, and God hears them, and only God understands and judges them, so one must be very careful with one's silences."

Yes, secrecy and its attendant, silence, can be forces for oppression and oppression's collaborators. Nevertheless, while secrecy can corrupt, all personal secrecy laid bare is not a formula for freedom but for totalitarianism and other forms of fanaticism. Fanaticism is predicated on controlling not only external actions but internal thought. In a totalitarian state, private life is official business. Our most treasured secrets belong to the state.

Yet we should not allow ourselves to forget that there can be a secret that doesn't denigrate or corrupt or victimize.

The bearing and revealing of a secret—isn't that the good secret of art? In art we may sense the presence of a secret that is not amenable to legislation and reduction. And the secret—the good secret, not the corrosive secrecy described in Adrienne Rich's collection of essays, *On Lies, Secrets, and Silence*—is what some of us want most as writers and as readers. We are drawn to novels, poems, short stories, drama and other art forms because each enacts experiences that are not entirely disclosed. Art is crafted to hold its secrets coiled. Writers speak across eras and cultures by bearing secrets.

The secret that stays secret is art.

Literature is the province of the secret, the unpeeling of a secret, the revelation and the return of a secret. It is even the place where a writer's secret may be that he feels every one else possesses the secret—and he or she doesn't, as John Updike has said Franz Kafka felt. Updike identifies what he calls Kafka's belief that everyone except himself had the secret [of happiness]. He received from his father an impression of helpless singularity, of being a "slave living under laws invented only for him." ... He felt, as it were, abashed before the fact of his own existence, "amateurish" in that this had never been quite expressed before. So singular, he spoke for millions in their new unease.

A secret is complex. In some contexts a secret is a burden, even a terror, but in other contexts, if chosen without fear and without expense to the innocent, a secret is a human right. We have a right to choose what we expose about ourselves. And the narrating or enacting of a secret is a means to create felt interiority, a heightened awareness of inwardness, as if an area of the psyche were sculpted out, reserved, and protected. To possess a secret in a story or poem or screenplay or other work of art is to know the power of a part of consciousness that is not policed or resists such policing. As the great writer and visual artist Bruno Schulz argued:

If art were merely to confirm what had already been established elsewhere, it would be superfluous. The role of art is to be a probe sunk into the nameless. The artist is an apparatus for registering processes in that deep stratum where value is formed. Destructive? But the fact that these contents express themselves as a work of art means that we affirm them, that our deep perception has spontaneously declared in their favor.

Art is a "probe" into the hidden and a manner of living within a metaphor of interiority and depths, of secret distances. A blow to our ability to respect our secrets is a blow to human capacity.

ξ

It doesn't seem debatable that our privacy—our sense of a secret and unexposed, interior world of our own—is increasingly vulnerable, not only when each person's privacy may be violated but when the opportunity to create what might be called the inner life, with all its imaginative potential, receives so little respect. Increasingly, against our will, our location can be traced, our patterns of consumption tallied, our e-mail accounts surveyed, our identities stolen. Our supposedly private lives can be captured by audio recording or cell phone cameras or surveillance video and displayed on the Internet. Information about any of us, false or true, proliferates in more channels than ever before, and the experience of interiority and individual control is continually threatened. In the first chapter of this book I referred to "The Darling," Chekhov's story of a woman who only expresses others' opinions and never develops any of her own. Without an appreciation of how an inner world of imagination is rooted and nurtured and how private thoughts may be shaped and valued, ever more empty and malleable and miserable "darlings" come into being.

So much of life is a secret that wants to be expressed and can only be approximated. Experience resists words, which is why writers have work to do: to capture more ground, to register more impressions than have yet been realized in language. Beginning writers in particular are aware of the difficulty when they fail the language and complain, "Words can't express what I experienced." In some ways that sentiment is correct, and it would be naïve to say otherwise. Could Nabokov sketch the butterfly of that young writer's soul? Could Milton limn the territory of that young writer's private hell? Could Pirandello find enough characters to speak even one of the words that would suggest the very being of that young writer? Would Emily

Dickinson hear the funeral in her brain, because the funeral in that young writer's brain is louder? And the creator of Iago, even he, could he prick the yolk of that young writer's experience?

All the more reason for the writer of any age to try to express the inexpressible. Pride isn't speaking when writers make complaints about the inexpressible. Realism may be. But ambition should defy realistic expectations.

ξ

Mario Vargas Llosa writes in the most direct way regarding an essential secret that writers possess:

> [O]ne thing I am sure of amid my many uncertainties regarding the literary vocation: deep inside, a writer feels that writing is the best thing that ever happened to him, or could ever happen to him, because as far as he is concerned, writing is the best possible way of life, never mind the social, political, or financial rewards of what he might achieve through it.

I feel the same way. I can't help it; I am one of those people—I can't be alone—who wants to write after I'm dead.

The secret of having a secret life—and of gratitude for it—isn't exactly a secret if it's attested to. The irrepressible Henry Miller described in wonderfully grotesque terms what was involved in learning his craft and letting inspiration guide him:

> Such exquisite torture, this writing humbuggery! Bughouse reveries mixed with choking fits ... Squat images roped with diamond tiaras ... Balaam the ass licking his hind parts. Weasels spouting nonsense. A sow menstruating.

As he matured as a writer Miller maintained, "I learn less and realize more: I learn in some different, more subterranean way ... I eschew all clear cut interpretations: with increasing simplification the mystery heightens. What I know tends to become more and more unstateable."

A very different sort of writer than Miller, the meticulous stylist John Cheever describes in his journal "the thrill of writing ... the truly thrilling sense of this as an adventure; the hair, the grain of sand in one's mouth; the importance (but not at all a selfish one) of this exploration—the density of the rain forest, the shyness of the venomous serpents, the resounding conviction that one will, tomorrow, find the dugout and the paddle and the river that flows past the delta to the sea."

The near impossibility of conveying the mystery and exhilaration of making art drives writers to analogies that at first may seem extreme, but that to my mind (and probably to the minds of their authors), can only begin to express the phenomenon.

The Answer Is Mead

In 1072 as a bequest from Leofric, ninety-four riddle poems, some of the earliest surviving poems in Old English, were left to Exeter Cathedral. The riddles were probably written down in the year 970, according to translator and editor Michael Alexander, who has rendered the Exeter Riddles into vivid contemporary language. In his introduction to the poems, Alexander points out that "unstraightforwardness is common in Old English poetry as a whole, not only in the Riddles." He writes that the riddles "isolate a verbal indirectness—a guess-inviting quality—which is basic to the old vernacular poetry in general."

Try guessing the answer to the following:

> A man who tries to take me on,
> tests my strength, soon finds out,
> if his silly plan doesn't pall on him,
> that it is his back that will hit the dust …
>   … Guess my name
> who have such mastery of men on earth
> that I knock them about in broad daylight.

The solution to the riddle is printed somewhere in the text of this book.

Alexander's terms, "Unstraightforwardness" and "a guess-inviting quality," those are what much art exploits. To know the power of secrets is to tap some of the oldest human yearnings of both those who make riddles and those who yearn to decipher them.

Like riddles, jokes also invite us to guess where we might be led, but only after we first feel as if we're being misled. What follows are two lawyer jokes widely distributed on the Internet:

> Your attorney and your mother-in-law are trapped in a burning building. You only have time to save one of them. Do you: (1) have lunch?, or (2) go to a movie?
> — (*www.tcyonline.com*)

> A man was sent to Hell for his sins. As he was being taken to his place of eternal torment, he passed a room where a lawyer was having an intimate encounter with a beautiful young woman. "What a rip-off," the man muttered. "I have to roast for all eternity, and that lawyer gets to spend it with a beautiful woman." Jabbing the man with his pitchfork, the escort-

ing demon snarled, "Who are you to question that won
punishment?"

— *(VariousStuff.net)*

What's important in any joke is the up-rush of recognition that occurs after the punch line, as compressed subtextual connections arrive with the surprise of a possibly vulgar epiphany, but an epiphany no less. Secrets, jokes, and insults rely on narrative loading—and often on embarrassment, making what is culturally considered repugnant suddenly unavoidable. Jokes work by revealing envies, desires, and fears. Almost always, jokes threaten to reveal a secret.

When we talk about jokes we might say, "Did you get the joke?"— as if a joke could be physically handled, picked up, and carried, as if a joke must be something that we are responsible for retrieving. Given that many jokes are pressurized narratives, they have been routinely compared to poetry, which similarly depends on concision and a charged subtext.

There are few narratives more compressed than jokes and poems. As Robert Frost wrote in a notebook: "The Poem must have as good a point as a anecdote or a joke." The crafting of a secret in art is complex; it can't reveal itself immediately, but unfolds. Poetry may be a special case. A good poem comes stocked with secrets that are released without exhausting our sense of the poem's renewable power. (The line breaks in poetry are suspense marks—delay points until each secret panel of the poem opens.) Similarly, the structure of a joke works through conceptual embedding, and more often than not, as in the lawyer jokes quoted earlier, a violation of a fleshly boundary is at least implied.

In literature, never completely colonized by any principle or ideology, a secret propels plot and works like a long joke unfurled. Fiction aims toward revelation through the release of a core secret or a chain

errelated secrets. Literary plots stand in relation to memory as
nory stands in relation to a secret, for a secret is a bitten-off seg-
ent of the past. A bad secret is an embedded memory that insults
the mind. A good secret is an embedded memory that renews the
mind. Secrets are about the refusal of oblivion. About not forgetting.
The secret may be endlessly recycled—and in the process may lose
its connection to original fact. Its potency may change, but what it
retains is its status as an irritated memory.

Detective fiction offers a clarifying example of the power of
secrets in written art, and is the secret parent of much contempo-
rary literary fiction. Some of the mechanisms Agatha Christie em-
ployed aren't any less familiar to another sort of writer known, unlike
Christie, as an exquisite prose stylist: Ian McEwan. Both Christie
and McEwan fulfill what David Lehman calls "the contract between
the mystery writer and reader ... that life is an inexhaustible source
of curiosity and mystery and that we can survive the mysteries we
embrace." Isn't *Atonement* fashioned in some of its plot lines like an
Agatha Christie novel? The wrong man is fingered for a crime; there's
a precocious and unreliable witness and a dastardly couple. A child
lets her imagination run loose and sets in motion a series of horrible
complications. There's even a trick ending of sorts, although the trick
in McEwan's novel is more poignant than tricky.

The attitude promulgated through an exposure to detective fic-
tion is one of the most worthwhile attitudes to apply to reading—
and to a writer's revisions. It goes without saying that for discovery
(however muted) to take place, a secret must be threaded into the nar-
rative fabric. The narrative arc poses the work of excavation. As Frank
Kermode argued in *The Genesis of Secrecy*, secrecy is part of the very
stuff of stories: "What is the interpreter to make of secrecy consid-
ered as a property of all narrative, provided it is suitably attended to?"

During Agatha Christie's lifetime, the British talked about a
"Christie for Christmas" not only because the author was astonish-

ingly prolific on an annual basis but because she renewed the desire to traffic safely in uncovering ingenious secrets. We're lost and then found in each little fun house of her plots. We are rescued from our own anxieties as we weave our way through a narrative to discern a secret. Did those rice grains mean anything? The fish paste?

Creating a secret, hoarding a secret, delivering and revealing a secret, requires not just craft but stealth. Which is why writers are often cautioned by other writers to keep their plots secret before a manuscript has been completed. For excellent reasons: to evade withering mockery; to keep friends and relatives from stopping the writer dead in his or her tracks through their resentment. Friends and relatives, after all, are right to fear exposure, for so much that is not available to a writer's conscious awareness may be expressed as we write. Writers may be inadvertently betraying more secrets, including family secrets, than they recognize, which biographers realize all too well. (The best biographical treatment of a writer's family that I know of comes from Thomas Bailey Aldrich in *Ponkapog Papers:* "It would be idle to add the little we know about these persons to the little we know about Herrick himself. He is a sufficient problem without dragging in the rest of the family.")

The most compelling reason to keep writing-in-progress secret is to avoid ruining the story for ourselves, given that many writers, to sustain writing, need the sense of the impending, nearly implosive charge that secrecy provides. To write is to keep a secret from oneself, as the elves kept their secret from the shoemaker. We write, many of us, to discover a secret, feral and illicit, gestating beyond immediate awareness. Which is why a writer's secrets should earn the writer's respect. A dog buries its bone. A writer buries a complication. The work lives in us like a secret and matures. As James Richardson writes in *Vectors:* "We have secrets from others. But our secrets have secrets from us."

What Does a Secret Look Like?

In Joseph Conrad's short story "The Secret Sharer," an untested ship captain allows aboard a stowaway guilty of murder. At the story's conclusion, the captain endangers his ship and crew, nearly drawing the ship onto an island's rocks to allow the stowaway to slip overboard and swim to safety as "a free man, a proud swimmer striking out for a new destiny." Harboring a renegade, and keeping him secret, and then releasing him to his own devices, these acts enable the captain to contend with the depth of his own nature. The story can be read as ethical conundrum, as the captain's absorption of evil, as a capsule summary of maturation, as an adventure in the perils of leadership, or as a drama of erotic desire. Whatever reading we try, the narrative slides out of place, its secrets intact. As the captain recounts of the stowaway, "There was something that made comment impossible in his narrative, or perhaps in himself: a sort of feeling, a quality, which I can't find a name for." The captain, never himself named, becomes a double of the man he hides, until he risks himself and his ship to set the man free.

In the uncanny moment of first meeting between the captain and the stowaway, a secret is metamorphosed into a material body.

> The side of the ship made an opaque belt of shadow on the darkling glassy shimmer of the sea. But I saw at once something elongated and pale floating very close to the ladder. Before I could form a guess a faint flash of phosphorescent light, which seemed to issue suddenly from the naked body of a man, flickered in the sleeping water with the elusive, silent play of summer lightning in a night sky. With a gasp I saw revealed to my stare a pair of feet, the long legs, a broad livid back immersed right up to the neck in a greenish cadaverous glow. One hand, awash, clutched the bottom rung

of the ladder. He was complete but for the head. A head corpse! The cigar dropped out of my gaping mouth with tiny plop and a short hiss quite audible in the absolute stillness of all things under heaven. At that I suppose he raised up his face, a dimly pale oval in the shadow of the ship's side. But even then I could only barely make out down there the shape of his black-haired head. However, it was enough for the horrid, frostbound sensation which had gripped me about the chest to pass off. The moment of vain exclamations was past, too. I only climbed on the spare spar and leaned over the rail as far as I could, to bring my eyes nearer to that mystery floating alongside.

So this is what a secret looks like: ghostly, light-emitting, naked, crawling limb by limb, like "a headless corpse"—as if comprehension happens last for us, whereas first we feel the secret's presence as a brainless ghoul rising bit by bit out of the dead past. By degrees we become conscious of the power of this dim ghostly face. Recognizing the fullness of the form we at last lean forward to meet "that mystery floating alongside" our own lives.

"The Secret Sharer" is a composite of writerly acts, such as keeping a fugitive impulse, maintaining loyalty to that seemingly disreputable impulse despite not knowing its exact nature, and then, with great care as to timing, releasing the enigmatic secret. As in Conrad's story, any writer and reader may emerge as a secret sharer, and the printed page or illuminated screen may prove the medium for that compact. Then a reader harbors the writer, that second consciousness, and the reverse.

Dangerous and alluring, monsters are physical manifestations of secrecy. Art breeds monsters as catalytic secrets given physical form. It's essential that in Conrad's "The Secret Sharer" the harbored man is not guilty of a simple crime; he has murdered and thus is a sort of monster. Like the ship's captain in Conrad's story, writers must identify their own sources of violence, and must control and then deliberately allow the monstrous to escape. The writer, like both Mary Shelley and her Dr. Frankenstein, tries to create a living secret, often made piece-meal.

Think of vampires, those secrets that our daughters want to date. Monsters tend to fascinate adolescents, perhaps because adolescence is a period devoted to secrecy and to the difficult apprehension and development of an inner life. The vampire in a consumer culture is particularly intriguing, given that the ideal consumer—an adolescent girl whose desires are especially vulnerable to manipulation—becomes a figure worthy of being consumed. In vampire stories she is the object of the vampire's irrational desire, sought after with barely contained passion.

Vampires are a rebuke to life as we know it. They are eternal, never aging, mesmerizing, everything an adolescent may both long for and perceive as unattainable. Secret girlhood hungers that are stimulated and repressed and again stimulated are acted out through the vampire plot until the vampire exists, tantalizingly, as a secret sharer. Discussing the vampire book *Twilight* in *The Atlantic*, Caitlin Flanagan reprises her own girlhood and the secret world of adolescence that the novel awakened for her:

> Reading the book, I sometimes experienced what I imagined long-married men must feel when they get an unexpected glimpse at pornography: slingshot back to a world of sensa-

tion that, through sheer force of will and dutiful accep[tance]
of life's fortunes, I thought I had subdued.

Monsters—impure hybrids, secrets incarnate. Fantastic relics from childhood that still have the power to disturb.

Monsters make most of us want to look away at first. Gradually, they also make us want to look, and look harder.

The Vanishing Secret

To reveal a secret, first we must possess a secret.

There was always a secret. We were a secret. We were once, after all, children.

The facts of Rainer Maria Rilke's earliest years have been rehearsed often. This was a childhood in which he was alternately neglected or fantastically over-inscribed by parental desires, as William H. Gass describes the situation:

> Rilke's parents had lost a daughter the year before they begot Rene (as he was christened); hoping for another daughter to replace her, and until he was ready to enter school, his mother, Phia, got him up girlishly, combed his curls, encouraged him to call his good self Sophie, and handled him like a china doll, cooing and cuddling him until such time as he was abruptly put away in a drawer. Later, with a mournful understanding that resembled Gertrude Stein's, Rilke realized that someone else had had to die in order to provide him with a place in life.

absence circling upon an absence, Rilke's childhood was
...ed by parental allegiance to a dead child rather than to the actual
...ng child. Add this to the inevitable sense of incomprehension be-
queathed to any child and the result is potential estrangement many
times over.

Rilke remains the poet of the great enchantment and horror of
childhood. In his poem "Childhood," a child struggles to orient him-
self by counting men and women. He notices what other children
wear. He lists. He compares. What's large? What's small? What's the
same? Who matches the child? Who differs?

Rilke's "Childhood" has a pulse. Things move, glisten, grow.
Space and time open, widening to allow the child to recognize his
own separateness. The child gathers the emerging self in a time of
solitude, clutching the power of the circle of the self.

The child's toys are circular: ball, top, hoop. The circle of his face
disappears in a pond's circle, inscribing an inward movement, cutting
circles upon the mind. The poem's insistently repeated sound effects
and images of roundedness, its gardens and fountains, bring to mind
the many luminous rings of Rilke's poems, among them his Spanish
dancer, his carousel, his bowl of roses, as well as the pressured dy-
namism of animate roundedness, whirling, brimming, and rippling.

The child watches his sailboat until he sees other children's sail-
boats circling. He then forgets his own less beautiful sailboat, and
instead studies his reflection:

> ... the small pale
> face that sinking gazed out of the pond—:
> O childhood, O likeness gliding off ...
> To where? To where?

The final image of "Childhood" foretells anxieties: the child's
sense that his small craft (the poem and the identity that he longs to

perfect) must be compared to that of others and may be diminished in comparison. From its first stanza the poem has worried over difference. Nevertheless, the child's apprehension of difference is part of his rescue, a rescue achieved through the intensity of his own perceptions, and possibly the rescue of the child from being solely his parents' fantasy object.

Childhood, because of the extreme difference between the child self and the adult self, serves as a precursor for later disappearances. Rilke's images animate loss, the child's toy sailing ship and his own shining face circling upon the psyche and dissolving from sight.

Rilke's poems are intimate in a disturbing way. We may wish to remain passive but, as many readers have noted, the poems turn on us. We are being observed. A figure or object scrutinizes us. The reader is implicated by the startling final challenge of "Archaic Torso of Apollo," with its most appropriated, most irresistible ending line, "You must change your life." In its own terms, "Childhood" reveals a missed encounter—our failure to meet or wholly contain that ghost child we were, the one who glides off, bearing the cargo of childhood's secrets.

Rilke gives the impression of an intimacy not lost in translation, which may be why his poems are so frequently translated and why they are received with enduring gratitude even by readers who know him only in translation. His poetry survives translation, in part because the poems themselves are *about* translation, depicting the ways we struggle for meaning. It would seem that translation of one sort or another is their medium and part of their very message.

The final questions of "Childhood" are less plaintive than wondering, *"Wohin? Wohin?"* ("To where? To where?"). We might say that at some level this is the call of the abandoned child. More surely, it is the call of the being who has metamorphosed into adulthood and who knows that not only his childhood face has vanished but also a way of experiencing the world's largeness and strangeness. The

em's final cry is a repeated question that resonates with awe more
han with grief—and it is one source of a writer's power, the secret
of translating the loss of a state of mind and body from that secret
kingdom of childhood, a secret that is shared with readers, if they'll
let themselves remember.

Poetry, Defended. Briefly.

In considering secrecy and ambition, I'll refer to several poems, for
poetry is the medium of a particular intensity, of intimations that
defy the language we use to express them. As a genre poetry keeps
defending its secrets and insisting that the reader or listener become a
secret bearer of sorts. Much of contemporary poetry remains mark-
edly ambitious—sometimes almost untenably—in the demands it
places on readers.

There are questions that we should confront: How can we live
in the midst of a reality that outpaces our ability to comprehend
it? How can the ancient springs of poetry—rhythmic language
shaped to be remembered, language that often assumes nature as
inspiration—survive in circumstances that disintegrate memory and
nature, a culture in which there is too much to remember and a sur-
plus of unnatural stimuli that clamors for our attention, but that may
not be worth remembering? And why should a writer choose to write
poetry, which baffles certain narrative impulses and remains under-
read and under-valued as a genre, if we judge value by attention given
within a culture?

One possible answer: poetry makes palpable the psychic pressure
of heightened contemporary experience, presenting in an imagisti-
cally associative manner the impression of living at a rate and a speed
that other genres may not readily supply. Poetry refills our felt sense
of interiority. Poetry demands that we place sustained pressure on

our imaginative and linguistic resources, that we call up mental ages of a sometimes incredible density, that we actively attend to both the shapes of mayhem and the shapes of controlled order as they are enacted in language. That is, in poetry more than in any other verbal genre, readers bring an expectation that not only do all elements matter down to the comma and the white space at the end of a line and between or within stanzas, but that each of those elements, no matter how widely arrayed, may tug at other elements and condition the whole. The poem is an echo chamber where we listen to the reverberations that otherwise dissolve into the white noise of anxiety.

For all the innovations that we speak of in poems, the genre remains the one where space and time are most acutely accented and where expectations of concentrated attention are most sought. The medium may mimic both the quick-order changes that bedevil us in our present landscape and the way certain brutal facts cannot be transformed but can be addressed despite what Wole Soyinka calls "the shrinking ethical space that is still left for humanity."

Death Is Not the Mother of Beauty

If the good secret of art intimates disappearances in time, this kind of secrecy also opens areas that stimulate the sensation of both moving toward understanding and failing at understanding.

In David Markson's novel *Vanishing Point,* an author, troubled by failing health, gathers and organizes a compendium of anecdotes, quotations, and unusual facts as a tentative stay against his losses. One statement he collects draws me up short: "Paul Celan was apparently comfortable in translating verse from no fewer than eight languages." I am moved by Celan's facility, and by his determination to transport meaning across the borders of many languages. Despite the temptation to disengage from translating the incomprehensible

e of human suffering, Celan is an advocate for speech, but it is
articularly demanding speech that he advocates in any language:
speech attuned to betrayal and to secrecy—and to conveying inti-
mations through time. As Celan writes, "[A] poem is not timeless.
Certainly it lays claim to infinity, it seeks to reach through time—
through it, not above and beyond it"—and thus not above or beyond
Celan's own endurance of forced labor in Romanian work camps, and
the disappearance of his parents into a concentration camp where
they were murdered. At times we may be taken by the way Celan's
poetry is abetted by lyric traces of what might be called beauty, but it
is impossible to imagine Celan saying with Wallace Stevens, "Death
is the mother of beauty."

It is hard not to read a poem like "Speak You Too" as a prophecy
of Celan's suicide in its final image of a poet, standing on a reduced
platform, exposed and vulnerable: "Thinner you grow, less knowable,
finer!" Such an image resonates with those in his "Speech on the Oc-
casion of Receiving the Literature Prize of the Free Hanseatic City
of Bremen" in which Celan argues that the "ways of thought" in his
poetry "are the efforts of someone who, overarced by stars that are
human handiwork, and who, shelterless in this till now undreamt-of
sense and thus most uncannily in the open, goes with his very being to
language, stricken by and seeking reality." In the imagination the body
may become as fine and barely visible as a thread, but a thread upon
which both the known and the unknown travel, where something
never before apprehended may find a route to us.

In Paul Celan's poems, words return and announce their repeti-
tiveness, as filaments between stanzas and across contraries. Like a
riddle, his poems keep opposing terms circulating, for Celan suggests
that what isn't a riddle isn't speaking. The furthest speech of poetry,
for Celan, must enclose the deepest contradictions and must be made
of what refuses the norms of expression.

Celan won't allow the mind to rest, sloughing off assured knowl-

edge and instead dramatizing mental processes that resist c̶ ̶
ment. In less extreme circumstances, such an impetus toward ̶
tion can be a motive force for poetry: the refusal to be anyone's pr̶
Celan's poetry unties referents until a conceptual system is lifted by
the corners. To make one claim is to bring its opposite into the open.
He urges us to make our claims without betraying the riddle of what
we are—beings whose origin and end we can only begin to imagine.

Secrets Work Their Way Through Us

"I'll let you in on a secret. One's deepest secret / is a certainty that
protects against the world."

Those are the words of the writer and law professor Lawrence
Joseph, whose poems are made of condensed narratives that depend
on heightened references to the vulnerabilities of the body. As Joseph
insists, "that's the law. To bring to light / most hidden depths." His
poems embody and reflect on what he calls "pressure"—the invisible
psychic elements of our contemporary situation. As a writer he pro-
tects our sense of the interior life, the "concealed things, sweet sleep
of colors" and then, at precise intervals, allows interior violations to
be revealed: "The point is to bring / depths to the surface, to elevate
/ sensuous experience into speech and the social contract."

In Don DeLillo's novel *Falling Man* a man who escaped from in-
side one of the towers of the World Trade Center on September 11,
2001, arrives at an emergency room. A medical technician picks glass
out of the man's face and begins to talk about the after-effects of
suicide bombings:

> In those places where it happens, the survivors, the people
> nearby who are injured, sometimes, months later, they de-
> velop bumps, for lack of a better term, and it turns out this

s caused by small fragments, tiny fragments of the suicide bomber's body. The bomber is blown to bits, literally bits and pieces, and fragments of flesh and bone come flying outward with such force and velocity that they get wedged, they get trapped in the body of anyone who's in striking range. Do you believe it? A student is sitting in a café. She survives the attack. Then, months later, they find these little, like, pellets of flesh, human flesh that got driven into the skin. They call this organic shrapnel.

In the technician's account, pieces of the body—now a corpse—of the murderer-suicide are lodged in the innocent bystander's living body. She is inhabited by the bomber's flesh, and that dead flesh will eventually rise to the surface of her living skin.

In much of Joseph's poetry a narrative of violated flesh emerges. The psychic pressure of recalled and predicted violence in the United States and in the Middle East occupies poems as explicit subject matter or as a constituent of formal organization in which fragments of embedded particulars—narrative accounts, bits of dialogue, references from numerous sources—are made dynamic, as in DeLillo's account of the "pellets" of bombed flesh that bury themselves but eventually "develop," revealing themselves in a living human body. In Joseph's poems the dead past enters the living and "works" its way into the present and into intimations of the future. The past and our re-imagining of the past, and our speculations about the future, are thereby not suspended but circulate. What was once secret reveals itself. We can read one of Joseph's lines, "I don't know about you, but it all goes through my skin" for a direct example of how experience in Joseph's poem is rendered as both physically embedded and volatile. The perpetration of violence and the perpetrators themselves burrow within the poems' structures and within their speakers' psyches.

Joseph reminds us that we cannot escape one another. Bodies, no

matter how apparently free or unviolated. affect other bodies. In h
poem "Unyieldingly Present," a scene of violence is refracted into
sensations of pressure, as violence is "encoded in the brain." The
syntax of language and the syntax of history are obsessively dwelled
upon as Joseph engages in "The act of forming / imagined language
resisting humiliation." The result is writing that works through a pro-
cess of embedding and subsequent eruptions.

I've chosen the word *embedded* as only a partial, but I hope resonant,
description of a dominant element in Joseph's poems and in the way
the intimation of a secret private interior proves significant in our
perception of written art. That is, one method by which the secret of
art works is to enact the manner in which the psyche embeds trauma.

The American Heritage Dictionary gives as primary definitions of *embed*:
"To fix firmly in a surrounding mass"; "To enclose snugly or firmly";
"To cause to be an integral part of a surrounding whole"; "To assign
(a journalist) to travel with a military unit during an armed conflict";
and, from biology, "To enclose (a specimen) in a supporting mate-
rial before sectioning for microscopic investigation." Each definition
takes on metaphorical life in Joseph's poetry.

Tellingly, his collection following 9/11 is titled *Into It*. A trouble-
some pronoun, "it" is ungendered, used ambiguously for singular or
plural, for the living or non-living. The preposition "Into" designates
an immersion—whether into Dante's inferno or a traffic jam; into
Henry James's "the world of creation" (cited in Joseph's epigraph
to *Into It*); or, given this poet's preoccupations, into an interior deci-
mated by 9/11.

During the early days of the Iraq war the term *embedded* took on
re-directed usage with the advent of embedded correspondents, news
reporters who traveled with military troops and were protected by
troops. Whatever one thinks of the ethics or the outcome of this

ctice, in relation to news reporting the term has come to suggest desire for authenticity and, at the same time, an ambiguous and suspect position—a witness to immediate effects of combat and yet a witness whose objectivity may have been sacrificed. The phrase *embedded correspondent* assumes a metaphorical complexity if applied to Joseph's poetry, for he is a poet seeking lines of correspondence, while he takes a position that differs markedly from that of the embedded news reporter, given that Joseph so thoroughly complicates notions of what it means to report or to witness an event.

Elaine Scarry has written about an abstract quality that Joseph puts into circulation next to violence: beauty. She argues that beauty and justice are interrelated, and that an awareness of beauty spurs an urge toward generative activity. As Scarry writes, "Beauty brings copies of itself into being. It makes us draw it, take photographs of it, or describe it to other people." But I would argue that, so too, in Scarry's own language, does violence "[bring] copies of itself into being. It makes us draw it, take photographs of it, or describe it to other people." The reverberant images of lyric poetry are embedded in Joseph's poetry. Lilacs, bridges, poplars, the sea, roses, the moon, a garden, the harbor, a marriage are called up. Such images of beauty move us momentarily beyond devastation, and yet we are soon again enfolded in a reality that Wole Soyinka has described aptly as contemporary fate:

> Constantly immersed in the cumulative denigration of human sensibilities, only to have one's most pessimistic predilections topped again and again by new acts—or revelations—of the limitless depth to which the human mind can sink in its negative designs.

In contemporary poetry, the perception of the body's vulnerability is acute. As Wisława Szymborska insists in her poem "Torture,"

the mind and spirit may travel, but the body "is and is and is / and r
no place to go." Or, as Joseph says in the poem "Rubaiyat":

> I want you to watch carefully
> what I am saying now—are you
> with me? An inch-long piece of steel,
> part of the artillery shell's
>
> casing, sliced through the right eye
> into his brain, severely damaging
> the optic nerve of his left eye,
> spraying bone splinters
>
> into the brain, making him quick to lose
> his temper, so acutely sensitive to pain
> the skin on his face hurts
> when wind blows against it . . .

In a period when explanatory structures are sliding away from comprehension, or are so reductive as to have little bearing on our lived experience, Joseph writes poems that embed evidence of the accumulated trauma of generations and the condensed experience of contemporary reality. Giorgio Agamben in *The End of the Poem* argues that poetry "tenaciously lingers and sustains itself in the tension and difference between sound and sense." We can adjust that supposition and add that poetry inserts itself in the realm between silence and non-sense. Joseph's poems are tense with the possibility that an affront to sense and meaning, in the form of senseless violence, may intrude at any moment. Emily Dickinson's challenge to us to "dwell in Possibility" takes on a new cast; Joseph suggests we are dwelling in possibilities of endless violence.

In his essay "The Targets of Aggression," David P. Barash refers to studies in which a rat in an electrified cage is shocked repeatedly. Eventually the rat succumbs to its miserable situation. As Barash explains, "When autopsied, the animal will be found to have oversized adrenal glands and, frequently, stomach ulcers, both indicating serious stress." What is surprising about the experiment is what happens if the rat has access to a stick.

If the rat gnaws on a stick during the period when the shocks are being administered, an autopsy will show a smaller number of ulcers and less enlarged adrenal glands than those in the autopsy of the rat denied the stick. In the final stage of this gruesome experiment, two rats share the electrified cage. When shocked, they do not grow apathetic but fight each other. Barash tells us, "[A]t autopsy, their adrenal glands are normal, and, moreover, even though they have experienced numerous shocks, they have no ulcers." His conclusion? "When animals respond to stress and pain by redirecting their aggression outside themselves, whether biting a stick or, better yet, another individual, it appears that they are protecting themselves from stress." As Barash argues, "When an individual suffers pain, he most often responds by passing it on to someone else. When possible, that 'someone else' is the perpetrator, the original source of the pain. But if this cannot be achieved, then others are liable to be victimized, regardless of innocence." Pain is passed on for reasons that are at least partly biological.

If the experiment's implications can be applied to humans, the findings suggest that our biology urges us to take our problems out on others, that such urges run rampant unless channeled, and that punishing wrongdoing is a biological need and difficult to manage. We tend to overcompensate. We may be prone to "redirect[ing] aggression," finding scapegoats and assigning guilt even to the inno-

cent. In what appears to be a related insight, Theodore Ziolkows
points out that the biblical injunction to extract "an eye for an eye
was originally meant to curb excessive violence by insisting that only
equivalent violence be enacted: break my arm and I break your arm,
but I don't wipe out your entire family.

If telling stories is one of our ways "to chew on a stick," then the
more stressful our reality, the more we need stories that allow us to
increase our awareness of whatever electrified cage we happen to be
in. And the more ambitious we need to be to invent such stories.

Ambition's Secret

What does written art ask of us as writers and as readers? That we
seek secrecy, its vibrations, intuiting the future and the hidden cur-
rents that sway the present. For many writers, ambition involves mak-
ing a counter-reality that gives the impression of defeating something
close to panic. Making a secret, that most compressed emblem of
the inner life, is a way to intensify the sensation of being alive. Think
of Wallace Stevens, who had the wit and Emersonian self-belief to
begin a poem: "It is the word *pejorative* that hurts" ("Sailing After
Lunch"). Stevens wrote with a sense of bearing a secret, and he wrote
sometimes—some readers would say—as if in code. He famously
argued: "Poetry must resist the intelligence—almost successfully." So
must our secrets, the secret agents of art.

We don't need anyone to do our worrying for us, but we do need
new imaginings that are deeper than anxiety and that sustain us by
respecting the depth of both other lives and our own.

ξ

Virginia Woolf in the short story "An Unwritten Novel" might be speaking for all writers:

> Wherever I go, mysterious figures, I see you, turning the corner, mothers and sons; you, you, you. I hasten, I follow ... If I fall on my knees, if I go through the ritual, the ancient antics, it's you, unknown figures, you I adore; if I open my arms, it's you I embrace, you I draw to me—adorable world!

The writer enters rapturously into writing, responding both to the known world and to the unknown world that waits to be written into being. To be able to do so—to continue over years to do so—should be the highest ambition of all. It's a truism to say that any writer is blessed who honors the impulse to write (and faithfully follows that impulse), and that the impulse and its fulfillment through the act of writing itself are the indications of ambition, if not the testimony of success. Of course truisms earn our suspicion.

Except that this one deserves to be true.

BIBLIOGRAPHY

Agamben, Giorgio. *The End of the Poem: Studies in Poetics*. Translated by Daniel Heller-Roazen. Stanford: Stanford University Press, 1999.

Aldrich, Thomas Bailey. *Ponkapog Papers*. http://www.online-literature.com/thomas-bailey-aldrich/ponkapog/18/.

Alexander, Michael. "The Exeter Riddles." In *The First Poems in English*. New York: Penguin, 2008. 9–29.

Alvarez, A. *The Writer's Voice*. New York: Norton, 2004.

Amis, Kingsley. *Lucky Jim*. New York: Penguin, 1953.

Amis, Martin. "He took the novel onto another plane of intimacy." *The Guardian*, January 28, 2009. http://www.guardian.co.uk/books/2009/jan/28/johnupdike-usa/.

—. *The Second Plane, September 11: Terror and Boredom*. New York: Knopf, 2008.

Auden, W. H. *The Dyer's Hand and Other Essays*. New York: Random House, 1962.

—. "Thanksgiving for a Habitat." In *W. H. Auden: Selected Poems*. Edited by Edward Mendelson. New York: Vintage, 2007. 262–273.

Austen, Jane. *Northanger Abbey*. New York: Vintage, 2007.

Babel, Isaac. "You Must Know Everything." In *You Must Know Everything: Stories 1915–1937*. New York: Carroll & Graf, 1969. 5–12.

Barash, David P. "The Targets of Aggression." *The Chronicle Review*, Section 5, October 5, 2007, B6–B9.

Barnes, Julian. *Nothing To Be Frightened Of*. New York: Knopf, 2008.

Baum, L. Frank. *The Wonderful Wizard of Oz: Centennial Edition*. New York: ibooks, 2001.

Bellow, Saul. *Humboldt's Gift*. New York: Avon, 1975.

Berryman, John. *The Dream Songs*. New York: Farrar, Straus and Giroux, 1969.

Bishop, Elizabeth. "Poem." In *Geography III*. New York: Farrar, Straus and Giroux, 1976. 36–39.

Bok, Sisela. *Secrets: On the Ethics of Concealment and Revelation*. New York: Vintage, 1983.

Bolaño, Roberto. *By Night in Chile*. Translated by Chris Andrews. New York: New Directions, 2003.

Borges, Jorge Luis. *This Craft of Verse*. Edited by Calin-Andrei Mihailescu. Cambridge: Harvard University Press, 2000.

Bradbury, Ray. "Because, Because, Because, Because, Because of the Wonderful Things He Does." In *The Wizard of Oz: Centennial Edition*. New York: ibooks, 2001. 41–49.

Brontë, Charlotte. "Biographical Notice of Ellis and Acton Bell." In *Wuthering Heights*, by Emily Brontë. New York: Barnes & Noble, 2004. xxix–xxxvi.

Carroll, Lewis. *Alice's Adventures in Wonderland and Through the Looking Glass*. New York: Signet, 2000.

Carson, Anne. "Dirt and Desire: Essay on the Phenomenology of Female Pollution in Antiquity." In *Men in the Off Hours*. New York: Knopf, 2000. 130–57.

—. "The Glass Essay." In *Glass, Irony and God*. New York: New Directions, 1995. 1–38.

Cavafy, C. P. *Collected Poems*. Translated by Edmund Keeley and Philip Sherrard. Edited by George Savidis. Princeton: Princeton University Press, 1992.

Celan, Paul. "Speak You Too." In *Selected Poems and Prose of Paul Celan*. Edited and translated by John Felstiner. New York: Norton, 2001. 77.

Chekhov, Anton. "The Darling." In *Ward No. 6 and Other Stories*. New York: Barnes & Noble, 2003. 247–259.

Cheever, John. *The Journals of John Cheever*. New York: Knopf, 1991.

Christie, Agatha. *Five Complete Novels of Detection: Ten Little Indians, Peril at End House, The Murder at Hazelmoor, Easy to Kill, Evil Under the Sun*. New York: Avenel, 1986.

"Col. Prentiss Ingraham." *Mississippi Writers & Musicians*. *www.mswritersandmusicians.com/ writers/prentiss-ingraham.html*.

Compton-Burnett, Ivy. *A House and Its Head*. New York: New York Review Books, 2001.

Conrad, Joseph. "The Secret Sharer." In *Heart of Darkness & The Secret Sharer*. New York: Signet, 1910. 19–61.

Corn, Alfred. *The Poem's Heartbeat: A Manual of Prosody*. Port Townsend: Copper Canyon, 2008.

DeLillo, Don. *Falling Man*. New York: Scribner, 2007.

Dickinson, Emily. *The Complete Poems of Emily Dickinson*. Edited by Thomas H. Johnson. New York: Little, Brown, 1960.

Duras, Marguerite. *Writing*. Translated by Mark Polizzotti. Minneapolis: University of Minnesota Press, 2011.

Eliot, George. *Middlemarch: A Study of Provincial Life*. New York: Signet, 2003.

Epstein, Joseph. "Duh, Bor-ing." *Commentary*, June 2011. *www.commentarymagazine.com/ article/duh-boring/*.

Faulkner, Robert. *The Case for Greatness: Honorable Ambition and Its Critics*. New Haven: Yale University Press, 2007.

Fenton, James. "The Gene-Pool." In *Out of Danger*. New York: Farrar, Straus and Giroux, 1994. 101.

—. Untitled. In *Out of Danger*. 96.

Fisher, M. F. K. *The Art of Eating*. New York: Vintage, 1954.

—. *A Life in Letters: Correspondence*. Washington, D.C.: Counterpoint, 1997.

Fitzgerald, F. Scott. *The Crack-Up*. Edited by Edmund Wilson. New York: New Directions, 1945.

—. *The Great Gatsby*. New York: Macmillan, 1980.

Flanagan, Caitlin. "What Girls Want." *The Atlantic*, December 2008, 108, 110–114, 116–118, 120.

Flaubert, Gustave. *Madame Bovary*. Translated by Paul DeMan. New York: Norton, 1965.

Frame, Janet. *An Autobiography*. New York: Braziller, 1989.

Franzen, Jonathan. "No End to It: Rereading *Desperate Characters*." In *Desperate Characters*, by Paula Fox. New York: Norton, 1999. vii–xiv.

Freud, Sigmund. *Jokes and Their Relation to the Unconscious*. Translated by James Strachey. New York: Norton, 1960.

Frost, Robert. *The Notebooks of Robert Frost*. Edited by Robert Faggen. Cambridge: Belknap Press of Harvard University Press, 2006.

Gass, William H. *Reading Rilke: Reflections on the Problem of Translation*. New York: Basic Books, 2000.

Goodstein, Elizabeth B. *Experience Without Qualities: Boredom and Modernity*. Stanford: Stanford University Press, 2005.

Hall, Donald. "Poetry and Ambition." In *Breakfast Served Any Time All Day: Essays on Poetry, New and Selected*. Ann Arbor: University of Michigan Press, 2003. 154–170.

Hass, Robert. *Twentieth Century Pleasures: Prose on Poetry*. New York: Ecco, 2000.

Hensher, Philip. "The play's the thing ... unless you're a novelist." *The Guardian*, July 26, 2006, *www.guardian.co.uk/stage/2006/jul/26/theatre/*.

Hollinghurst, Alan. *The Stranger's Child*. New York: Knopf, 2011.

Hopkins, Gerard Manley. "God's Grandeur." In *Mortal Beauty, God's Grace: Major Poems and Spiritual Writings of Gerard Manley Hopkins*. Edited by John F. Thornton and Susan B. Varenne. New York: Vintage, 2003. 21.

Ingalls, Rachel. *Mrs. Caliban*. New York: Laurel, 1983.

James, Henry. "The Art of Fiction." In *Criticism: Major Statements*, fourth edition. Edited by Charles Kaplan and William Davis Anderson. New York: Bedford, 2000.

—. *The Turn of the Screw*. New York: Norton, 1999.

Jiménez, Juan Ramón. *The Complete Perfectionist: A Poetics of Work*. Edited and translated by Christopher Maurer. Chicago: Swan Isle, 2011.

Jin, Ha. *The Writer as Migrant*. Chicago: University of Chicago Press, 2008.

Joyce, James. *Ulysses*. New York: Random House, 1961.

Joseph, Lawrence. *Codes, Precepts, Biases, and Taboos: Poems 1973–1993*. New York: Farrar, Straus and Giroux, 2005.

—. *Into It: Poems*. New York: Farrar, Straus and Giroux, 2005.

—. "Working Rules for *Lawyerland*." *Columbia Law Review* 2001, 101.

Kafka, Franz. *Letters to Friends, Family, and Editors*. Translated by Richard and Clara Winston. New York: Schocken, 1977.

Keats, John. "When I Have Fears That I May Cease to Be." In *Selected Poems and Letters*. Edited by Douglas Bush. Boston: Houghton Mifflin, 1959.

Kermode, Frank. *The Genesis of Secrets*. Cambridge: Harvard University Press, 1979.

Kinzie, Mary. "Introduction: The Dance of Creation." In *The Sea, The Sea*, by Iris Murdoch. New York: Penguin, 2001. vii–xxvi.

Kirn, Walter. "Boredom is Extinct." *The Atlantic*, July/August 2010, 52.

Kundera, Milan. *Ignorance*. Translated by Linda Asher. New York: HarperCollins, 2002.

Lamb, Charles and Mary. "Cleanliness." In *The Works of Charles and Mary Lamb*. Edited by E. V. Lucas. New York: Putnam, 1903. 363–64.

Larkin, Philip. "Dockery and Son." In *Collected Poems*. New York: Farrar, Straus and Giroux, 2003. 108–109.

aw Humor." TCY Online. www.tcyonline.com/law/law_fingmatters.php/.

ehman, David. *The Perfect Murder: A Study in Detection.* New York: Macmillan, 1989.

Llosa, Mario Vargas. *Letters to a Young Novelist.* Translated by Natasha Wimmer. New York: Farrar, Straus and Giroux, 2002.

Lorca, Federico García. "Floating Bridges." In *Collected Poems.* Edited by Christopher Maurer. New York: Farrar, Straus and Giroux, 2002. 405.

Lowell, Robert. Introduction. In *Ariel*, by Sylvia Plath. New York: Harper and Row, 1966. xiii–xvi.

Marlowe, Christopher. *Dr. Faustus.* New York: Broadview, 2007.

Marr, David. "Patrick White's Return from the Pit." *Sydney Morning Herald*, November 3, 2006, *www.smh.com.au/news/books/patrick-whites-return-from-the-pit/2006/11/02/1162339990980.html/.*

Martin, Agnes. *Writings.* Edited by Dieter Schwarz. Kuntsmuseum Winterthur/ Edition Cantz, 1992.

Max, D. T. "The Unfinished: David Foster Wallace's project." The *New Yorker*, March 9, 2009, 48–61.

McEwan, Ian. *Atonement.* New York: Vintage, 2002.

McGrath, Charles. "Norman Mailer, Towering Writer with Matching Ego, Dies at 84." *New York Times*, November 10, 2007, *www.nytimes.com/2007/11/10/books/11mailer.html/.*

Melville, Herman. *Moby-Dick, or, The Whale.* New York: Penguin, 2001.

Milhauser, Steven. "Dangerous Laughter." In *Dangerous Laughter.* New York: Knopf, 2008.

Miller, Henry. *Henry Miller on Writing.* New York: New Directions, 1964.

Miłosz, Czesław. "Into the Tree." In *Unattainable Earth.* Translated by Czesław Miłosz and Robert Hass. New York: Ecco, 1986. 30–33.

Moore, Marianne. "Poetry." In *The Poems of Marianne Moore.* Edited by Grace Schulman. New York: Viking, 2003. 135.

Moravia, Alberto. *Boredom.* Translated by Angus Davidson. New York: New York Review Books, 1999.

—. *Conjugal Love.* Translated by Angus Davidson. London: Secker & Warburg, 1959.

Morton, Brian. *Starting Out in the Evening.* New York: Harvest, 2007.

Munro, Alice. "Haven." The *New Yorker* March 5, 2012, 66–73.

Murdoch, Iris. *The Black Prince.* New York: Penguin, 2003.

—. *The Sea, The Sea.* New York: Penguin, 2001.

Nabokov, Vladimir. *The Annotated Lolita.* Edited by Alfred Appel, Jr. New York: Random House, 1991.

Naipaul, V. S. "The Thing Without a Name." In *Miguel Street.* New York: Vintage, 1959. 15–21.

Nelson, Joshua B. "Humor Is My Green Card: A Conversation with Sherman Alexie." *WLT (World Literature Today)*, July/August 2010, 39–43.

Neruda, Pablo. "Some Thoughts on Impure Poetry." In *Passions and Impressions.* Translated by Margaret Sayers Peden. New York: Farrar, Straus and Giroux, 1983. 128-29.

Oates, Joyce Carol. "Notes on Failure." In *The Faith of a Writer.* New York: HarperCollins, 2003. 51–73.

O'Brien, Edna. *James Joyce: A Life.* New York: Penguin, 2011.

O'Connor, Flannery. *The Habit of Being: Letters of Flannery O'Connor.* Edited by Sally Fitzgerald. New York: Farrar, Straus and Giroux, 1979.

Ozick, Cynthia. "Ghost Writers." *Pen America* 9, 2008, 139–141.

Pearl Poet. "Cleanness." In *The Pearl Poet: His Complete Works.* Translated by Margaret Williams. New York: Random House, 1967. 121–188.

Perkins, Maxwell. Letter to James Jones, May 28, 1947. In *Editor to Author: The Letters of Maxwell E. Perkins.* Edited by John Hall Wheelock. New York: Grosset & Dunlap, 1950.

Petre, Jonathan. "You Really Can Be Bored to Death, Scientists Discover." *Mail Online, Daily Mail,* United Kingdom, February 7, 2010.

Philips, Adam. *On Kissing, Tickling, and Being Bored: Psychoanalytic Essays on the Unexamined Life.* Cambridge: Harvard University Press, 1998.

Plath, Sylvia. *The Bell Jar.* New York: Harper, 1971.

—. "Fever 103." In *Ariel.* New York: Harper, 1999. 61–63.

—. "Lady Lazarus." In *Ariel.* 6–9.

Rich, Adrienne. *On Lies, Secrets, and Silence: Selected Prose, 1966–1978.* New York: Norton, 1979.

Richardson, James. *Vectors: Aphorisms & Ten-Second Essays.* Keene, New York: Ausable, 2001.

Rilke, Rainer Maria. "Childhood." In *The Book of Images.* Translated by Edward Snow. San Francisco: North Point, 1991. 40–43.

—. "The Panther." In *The Book of Fresh Beginnings: Selected Poems of Rainer Maria Rilke.* Translated by David Young. Oberlin: Oberlin College Press, 1994. 44.

Robinson, Marilynne. Interview. "The Art of Fiction Number 198." *Paris Review* 186, Fall 2008, 37–66.

—. *When I Was a Child I Read Books.* New York: Farrar, Straus and Giroux. 2012.

Roethke, Theodore. "Dolor." In *The Collected Poems of Theodore Roethke.* New York: Anchor, 1974.

Rushdie, Salman. *The Wizard of Oz.* London: British Film Institute, 1992.

Scarry, Elaine. *On Beauty and Being Just.* Princeton: Princeton University Press, 1999.

Schulz, Bruno. "An Essay for S. I. Witkiewicz (1935)." In *Polish Writers on Writing.* Edited by Adam Zagajewski. San Antonio: Trinity University Press, 2007. 31–35.

Schweizer, Harold. *On Waiting.* London: Routledge, 2008.

"Shakespearean Insults" at *www.william-shakespeare.org.uk/shakespeare-insults-xyz.htm/.*

Shelley, Mary. *Frankenstein.* New York: Bantam, 1981.

Smith, Zadie. "That Crafty Feeling." *The Believer* (June 2008): 5–12.

Soyinka, Wole. *Climate of Fear: The Quest for Dignity in a Dehumanized World.* New York: Random House, 2005.

Spacks, Patricia Meyer. *Boredom: The Literary History of a State of Mind.* Chicago: University of Chicago Press, 1996.

Spark, Muriel. *The Finishing School.* New York: Doubleday, 2004,

—. *Loitering with Intent.* New York: New Directions, 1981.

—. *The Prime of Miss Jean Brodie.* New York: Harper, 1999.

—. "To the Gods of My Right Hand." In *All the Poems of Muriel Spark.* New York: New Directions, 2004. 51.

—. "You Should Have Seen the Mess." In *Open to the Public: New & Collected Stories.* New York: New Directions, 1985. 141–46.

Steiner, George. *My Unwritten Books.* New York: New Directions, 2008.

Stevens, Wallace. "Of Modern Poetry." In *Collected Poetry and Prose.* New York: Library of America, 1997. 218–219.

Svendsen, Lars. *A Philosophy of Boredom.* Translated by John Irons. London: Reaktion, 2008.

Szymborska, Wisława. "Torture." In *Miracle Fair: Selected Poems of Wisława Szymborska.* Translated by Joanna Trzeciak. New York: Norton, 2001. 46–47.

Tolstoy, Leo. *Anna Karenina.* Translated by David Magarshack. New York: Signet, 2002.

Toohey, Peter. *Boredom: A Lively History.* New Haven: Yale University Press, 2011.

Tranströmer, Tomas. "The Name." In *The Great Enigma: New Collected Poems.* Translated by Robin Fulton. New York: New Directions, 2006. 99.

Updike, John. Foreword. In *Franz Kafka: The Complete Stories.* New York: Schocken. 1971.

—. "Oz is Us: Celebrating the Wizard's Centennial." In *The Wizard of Oz: Centennial Edition.* New York: ibooks, 2001. 3–38.

"VariousStuff.net" at *http://jokes.variousstuff.net/.*

Vendler, Helen. Quoted in Rachel Donadio's "The Closest Reader." *New York Times Book Review,* December 10, 2006, *www.nytimes.com/2006/12/10/books/review/Donadio.t.html/.*

Vidal, Gore. "On Rereading the Oz Books." In *The Wizard of Oz: Centennial Edition.* New York: ibooks, 2001, 51–76.

Wallace, David Foster. *The Pale King.* New York: Little, Brown, 2011.

—. "Wiggle Room." The *New Yorker,* March 9, 2009, 63–66.

Warner, Marina. *Phantasmagoria: Spirit Visions, Metaphors, and Media into the Twenty-first Century.* Oxford: Oxford University Press, 2006.

Waters, John. *Role Models.* New York: Farrar, Straus and Giroux, 2010.

Waugh, Evelyn. *Vile Bodies.* New York: Back Bay, 1999.

Whitman, Walt. *Leaves of Grass.* New York: Signet, 1980.

Wiman, Christian. *Ambition and Survival: Becoming a Poet.* Port Townsend: Copper Canyon, 2007.

Wood, James. *How Fiction Works.* New York: Farrar, Straus and Giroux, 2008.

Woolf, Virginia. "An Unwritten Novel." In *Monday or Tuesday: Eight Stories.* Mineola, New York: Dover, 1997. 19–30.

—. *Moments of Being: A Collection of Autobiographical Writing.* Edited by Jeanne Schulkin. New York: Harvest, 1985.

Ziolkowski, Theodore. *The Mirror of Justice: Literary Reflections of Legal Crises.* Princeton: Princeton University Press, 1997.

Acknowledgments

I have been thinking about the issues that *Swallowing the Sea* explores for a number of years, and I am grateful to the following journals for publishing some of my initial reflections under the following titles: "The Bigamists: Writers Crossing Genres" *(Southwest Review;* later featured on the *Poetry Daily* website); "Embedded Chronicles: Lawrence Joseph's Poetry of Urgency" *(University of Cincinnati Law Review;* later featured on the *Jacket Magazine* website); "Purity: It's Such a Filthy Word" *(TriQuarterly;* later featured on the *Poetry Daily* website); "Why I Return to M. F. K. Fisher" (Ducts.org); "The Closest Work," "Trace Marks," and "What Isn't a Riddle Isn't Speaking" *(FIELD: Contemporary Poetry and Poetics).*

Willard Spiegelman of *Southwest Review* kindly suggested that I should add Robert Penn Warren to my list of representative writers who worked in multiple genres. I have taken his advice. Elizabeth Rosen encouraged me to submit remarks on M. F. K. Fisher to *Ducts.* The University of Cincinnati Law School published an essay of mine on Lawrence Joseph's poetry and held a symposium on his work that I was honored to participate in. I wish to thank Susan Firestone Hahn, who edited *TriQuarterly* and published my meditation on purity. The editors of *FIELD* have offered me multiple opportunities to sort out my thoughts, and I'm grateful. Stuart Friebert, David Walker, and David Young invited me to participate in symposia on Rainer Maria Rilke and Paul Celan. The portion of this book under the subheading "The Closest Work" derives from an essay first published in *FIELD* that later appeared in *Best Writing on Writing: Volume 2,* edited by Jack Heffron.

This book quotes many writers and their translators, to whom I owe immeasurable debts.

Grace Dane Mazur read my manuscript after I submitted it to Tupelo Press and passed it on to Jeffrey Levine with heart-stoppingly generous comments. I thank them for their support and for the brilliant ambition that their own writing conveys.

It is an exceptional piece of luck to have a poet as an editor. I am grateful for Jim Schley's extraordinary attentiveness and insight. This book is stronger than it would have been otherwise because of his care.

I thank Lafayette College and my colleagues and students, as well as Diane Shaw, our college archivist and a friend to all writers.

Members of my family appear in this book. They have inspired me with their independent minds, their exceptional humor, and their capacity for love. In this book I mention that my sister Lana and I used to play a game called *Who Can Think the Thought Never Thought Before.* When I first wrote about that game I had no idea that the unthinkable would occur in 2011 and we would lose her in this life. This book is dedicated to Lana's radiant spirit.

I thank my sister Alice Faye whose loyalty is unbounded. Together we hold close the memories of our mother and father, our brother Joe, and our sister Lana.

I thank my daughters Theodora and Cecilia who are, in every way, large and small, daily miracles. Finally, I thank Eric, my husband—courageous, stalwart, magnanimous companion of my heart.

CECE ZIOLKOWSKI

LEE UPTON *is the author of twelve books, including five collections of poetry, a novella, and four books of literary criticism. Her short stories have also appeared widely. Her awards include a Pushcart Prize, the National Poetry Series Award, two awards from the Poetry Society of America, and the Miami University Novella Award. She is Writer-in-Residence and a professor of English at Lafayette College.*